D0561153

OMNIVM LVX CIVIVM

BOSTON
PUBLIC
LIBRARY

LOVE'S COMPASS

Daniel Mark Epstein

LOVE'S COMPASS

A
NATURAL HISTORY
OF THE HEART

Addison-Wesley Publishing Company, Inc.

READING, MASSACHUSETTS   MENLO PARK, CALIFORNIA   NEW YORK
DON MILLS, ONTARIO   WOKINGHAM, ENGLAND   AMSTERDAM   BONN
SYDNEY   SINGAPORE   TOKYO   MADRID   SAN JUAN

Love's Compass is not a work of journalism or literal history. It is a book of meditations on the nature of love and the narrator's personal impressions. The incidents that appear in these pages are subjective representations of memories and opinions of the narrator. In some cases, the names, descriptions, and backgrounds of characters have been altered.

Library of Congress Cataloging-in-Publication Data

Epstein, Daniel Mark.
  Love's compass: a natural history of the heart / Daniel Mark Epstein.
        p.   cm.
      Includes index.
      ISBN 0-201-15667-9
      1. Love. 2. Friendship. 3. Parent and child. 4. Love—Religious aspects. 5. Love—Case studies. 6. Friendship—Case studies. 7. Parent and child—Case studies. 8. Love—Religious aspects—Case studies. 9. Epstein, Daniel Mark. I. Title.
BF575.L8E64   1990
128'.4—dc20   89-35069

Author photo by June Chaplin
Cover design by Lynn Breslin
Text design by Barbara DuPree Knowles
Set in 11½-point Garamond No. 3 by DEKR Corporation, Woburn, MA

ABCDEFGHIJ-DO-89
First printing, January 1990

In memory of my father
Donald David Epstein
1928–1988

Parts of this book appeared, in slightly different form, in *Gentleman's Quarterly, Baltimore Magazine,* and *The Philadelphia Inquirer Magazine.*

Comments on childhood friendship in Chapter Two are indebted to the writings of Jean Piaget and the laboratory work of Robert Selman of the Harvard School of Education. Paraphrasing of Plato's *Symposium* in Chapter Three draws upon the translations of W.H.D. Rouse and Benjamin Jowett.

For their help with this book, the author wishes to record his thanks to Rosemary Knower and Jane Isay.

CONTENTS

CONTENTS

CONTENTS

LOVE'S COMPASS

PREFACE

A MYSTERY

In my grandmother's house there was a vibration, recurrent and mysterious, like the diminishing echo of a cello chord. This sound was unmistakable to a boy of five, though it was so faint I could not be sure whether it was a real sensation or a memory.

What was its source?

The clapboard house stood at the edge of a tidewater town, miles from any cello. Besides, the vibration was less like any music than like the thrill that comes from certain music and is experienced not just with the ears but with the whole body. Later I would associate that sensation with the modal tunings of Appalachian stringed instruments—dulcimer, fiddle, and guitar—which seem to open unexpected passages in time.

I felt this sensation most often in the summer twilight when my grandfather was at work in the vegetable garden. Though I have called the house my grandmother's, it was equally my grandfather's, but it never seemed so. As many waking hours as she spent indoors, he spent outside in the garden, in all kinds of weather. He had been a sailor, shipping out from his home port of Rotterdam at the age of eleven. At twenty he gave up a life of adventure on the high seas to marry my grandmother. And I always had the feeling that the man had not quite *done* with his career as a sailor, that there had been some unfinished business, as he swaggered indoors and out, as if the house or the lawn beneath his feet might at any moment begin to list to port or starboard.

One of my earliest memories of my grandfather is of that powerful man striding up and down the yard in a night thunderstorm, his beaming face turned up toward the fresh rain, his silver hair irradiated by the lightning he defied to strike him. For twenty-five years he worked in the local power plant, and I think this must have given him a sense of acquired immunity to static voltage. In most things he was a moderate, prudent man, though he drank a little more whiskey than my grandmother approved, hiding a bottle in the garage rafters. Yet he believed the ozone liberated in lightning storms was as invigorating and regenerative a tonic for a man as for the trees and flowers.

If his own health could be admitted as evidence, my grandfather was right about the lightning, as he was about most things. He was as healthy and wise a man as I have ever known, a gentle pagan who had gotten his religious instruction from nature and the elements.

Yet it would never have occurred to me, on the calmest of summer nights, to ask my grandfather about the source of that gentle vibration that thrilled me—sometimes for as long as a whole minute as I watched the clock upon the piano. My grandfather could more easily explain the thunder. Nor would I ask my grandmother at twilight as she rocked me in the oak rocking chair across from the piano in the dining room. My grandmother was supremely logical, a southern Episcopalian, who could fry a rockfish or conduct the church rummage sale with breathtaking precision. Perhaps she could explain to me, in her musical Alabama accent, why the enormous upright piano had come to rest in the crowded dining room, dominating the space, instead of in the parlor where other families housed their pianos.

I investigated the piano, upon the suspicion the great harp of strings inside was creating, in silence, that sympathetic vibration. Even at five years of age, I understood that if the piano strings were causing the sensation it would be constant. It would not come and go that way, once a month, then two times in a week, haunting me in the pantry, then in the closet under the stairs. Next to the closet door there was an ancient oil painting of the head of Christ in the ecstasy of His torment under the crown of thorns—one of those portraits where the eyes now seem open and now closed. When the eyes were closed, I thought that the sound might be coming from under His eyelids.

I was amazed no one else ever mentioned the sound, for the feeling it inspired was so thrilling, though tinged with melancholy, coming and going. There was something nostalgic about it, palpable even to a child of five who has so little to look back on, some sense of the sweetness of return to an earlier and more pleasant condition, a resolution, a home. With a child's sense of secrecy, and property, ownership of a treasure that must diminish in the sharing, I kept the experience to myself. Perhaps there was a bit of bashfulness, too—the suspicion that any sensation so intensely pleasurable must in some way be shameful. As curious as I was to find the source, I would never risk asking anyone about it, even my mother who had grown up in the house, and from whom I concealed almost nothing.

So this remained a wellspring of private delight and speculation all through my youth and early manhood. Though I began to encounter the peculiar sensation in other places, it always remained most intense and in its purest state on the Eastern Shore of Maryland, in that house across the field from the tidal marsh with tall reeds and cattails. In my early teens, when I was old enough to speculate more forcefully about such things, I came to the conclusion that the vibration was caused by Time.

The house was not particularly old. It was one of those wood-frame houses popularly produced in the 1920s for the newly proliferating middle class. So in the 1950s the house was not more than a generation old. But the rooms were filled with old things: old books and pictures in gilt frames, antique furniture, ivory-colored lace doilies, and European crockery. My grandfather had come from Holland after World War I on one of his many tours as a merchant seaman. He met my grandmother in Mobile, Alabama, married her, and came to live in Vienna, Maryland, in the 1920s. But he maintained his family ties to the Old World. Returning from occasional voyages to visit his family in Holland, he would ship a cargo of relics: dark, heavily lacquered oil paintings of sixteenth-century interiors and brighter canvases of Dutch landscapes with windmills upon the canals, or blank-faced cattle, a seventeenth-century pier table with spindle legs and a rose marble top, and delicate crystal wine glasses that somehow managed to survive the transatlantic storms.

My grandmother's contributions to the household museum were mostly linens and beautifully colored quilts patchworked from scraps of nineteenth-century clothing. In the attic, most of the books my mother and her sister and brother had read in childhood—*Tom Swift and His Flying Machine, Robin Hood, Heidi,* the works of Cooper, Tennyson, and Scott—were piled upon a makeshift library table the length of the south wall, awaiting the next generation of bookworms. The books were generally younger than the house; but the dust upon them, and the silverfish that darted out of their pages, made them look ancient.

Downstairs, the living-room chairs and sofa where I sprawled to read Mark Twain or Dickens were overstuffed Victorian and Empire revival-style, with funny claw handles and feet that matched the carved oak of the dining-room table, the huge rocker. These furnishings were not old by the measure of a full lifetime. But to a boy visiting—a boy growing up in a brand-new, stainless steel, brick, and fiberboard housing development in the Washington suburbs—my grandmother's faraway home had the aura of some pre-Raphaelite's dream of a country castle.

So, my first working hypothesis about the source of the mysterious vibration was this: All these ancient and decaying things, having been handled and knocked around by my relatives since the dawn of Time, absorbed the life force of these people who had used and abused them. And once in a while the collection's energy, having risen to a critical level, would discharge itself into the atmosphere like a sigh of relief, wind through a ghostly wind chime, making a vibration nearly audible.

In these moments, which might be as brief as a few seconds or as long as a full minute, the visitor could experience Time, which is not the movement of the clock's hands or even the more visible swing of the pendulum. Time is the discharge of energy which re-establishes right equilibrium between human consciousness and the world of inanimate things.

Twilight, when day and night overlap, would provide a logical occasion for time to "back up" on itself in this fashion. The tidewater region, I reckoned, where land and sea merge, would provide a favorable atmosphere, a salty medium ripe for the perception of raw Time.

Now I realize this sort of thinking is not very scientific. In fact, it might seem like primitive nonsense to anyone used to dealing with material certainties. The answer to any essential human mystery, unlike the clever resolution of a detective mystery or a scientific problem, must always seem more or less primitive. The effort reminds us that, for all our modern learning, the outer limits of mortal knowledge do not really change. In view of the questions we might ask an approachable god, we are no wiser than our ancestors the savages.

In the absence of a better explanation, I first thought that the eerie vibration was Time, and I clung to that theory until I was well past the age of twenty. But in my mid-teens I began to experience longings that eventually would undermine the "Time" hypothesis, calling for an answer more in keeping with my broader experience.

I began to fall in love. Daydreaming of this girl or that girl, fantasizing about the moment of our ecstatic union, I imagined that I would transport her, by bicycle or bus, to the Eastern Shore of Maryland, to my grandmother's house. My grandparents would be gone for the evening, perhaps forever. There in the parlor the dreamgirl and I would sit, hand in hand, gazing out the window at the twilight. As the fireflies rose out of the ground and the stars came down out of the sky, the vibration would begin, the distant, sub-audible cello, and I would whisper to her: Can you feel it? And she would not need to speak, for I could tell from the look in her eyes she felt what I felt.

But not for another twenty years would I understand that the vibration in my grandparents' house was love. That is a conceptual understanding that had to be guided by an intuition, which then was nourished by a lot of reading and reflection. My grandparents were in love. They loved each other. They loved their children and grandchildren, and were loved in return, though probably not quite as much. Their children loved one another, the way sisters and brothers do. My grandfather and grandmother loved God, each in his or her own special and sometimes peculiar ways; and it will be the argument of this book that their love for God was reciprocated, in some graceful proportion.

It was not my grandparents' love for each other, or for their children, or for me, that made the air hum in the twilight. No particular expression or impression of love caused that vibration, but love itself, ever so briefly made perceptible. Love sounded a chord now and again, this chord of intense pleasure tinged with melancholy, to remind me that all of the component notes had been ringing there for generations. In visual terms, it was like noticing all at once that the rainbow of colors flowing from a prism is derived from a ray of pure sunlight.

THE MYSTERY AND
THE DOCTRINE OF LOVE

This book will investigate a fundamental human mystery, the mystery of love. It would be fruitless to go even a page further without a little more discussion of mystery, and of the mystical, which is where the mystery lives.

The word *mystical* puts many discerning readers on guard. And well it should, with its implications of bearded, stoned gurus, or sorcerers in dark robes embroidered with stars and moons, calling spirits from the vasty deep. Mysticism reminds us of mediums, faith healers, and tax-exempt cults that enslave gullible people by appealing to their superstitions, their primitive need to believe something—anything—however fantastic. Practical-minded people link mysticism, and the mystical, with balmy, rattle-brained behavior, as if mysticism had become an excuse for *not* thinking.

But mysticism—speculation upon themes as critical to life as they are incomprehensible—is certainly among the ultimate intellectual challenges.

Just as I was obsessed with discovering the source of that weird vibration in my grandmother's house, I am driven to try and understand the mysteries of the soul, love, and death, despite the comical odds against any success, despite the illustrious failures of great sages whose books line the walls of my study. Mysticism, when practiced by reasonable inquirers, is a no-holds-barred attempt to explain, through a combination of logic *and* intuition, one of the great mysteries, like the mystery of love or the mystery of gravity. In the twentieth century, once we have explained something, we call the explanation not mystical but scientific.

For the sake of illustration, let us briefly consider two famous mystical experiences: Saint Augustine's revelation in his Italian garden in 386, and Sir Isaac Newton's epoch-making collision with the apple in 1675.

I consider the physicist's moment as mystical as the saint's. Augustine, at the age of thirty-two, had put in twenty years of his life wrestling with the mystery of love. He was wracked with the question whether love might be celebrated and glorified in the flesh, in the old-fashioned pagan manner he so enjoyed, or whether love must be restricted to the pure spirit, as the Christians were insisting. This was, and continues to be, a burning question. In his *Confessions,* Augustine tells us he was "soul-sick and tormented" over the dilemma, and all his ingenious logic could not cure him.

Then one day Augustine was sitting in a Milanese garden with a friend, a celibate fellow a few years younger than himself. All of a sudden Augustine got up from the bench where he had been meditating, flung himself upon the ground under a fig tree, and burst into tears.

Out of nowhere came a childlike voice saying to Augustine: "Take it and read, take it and read." The Saint hurried back to where he had been sitting with his friend, who had been waiting all the while in silent wonder. The book, containing the Epistles of Saint Paul, lay on the bench. Augustine picked up the book and read the first passage his eyes fell upon: "Not in revelling and drunkenness, not in lust and wantonness . . . rather, arm yourself with the Lord." Apparently this was all Saint Augustine needed to hear. He had had a mystical experience. He would have no more of pagan lechery ever again. He went back into the house and told his mother (who was already a Christian) that he was ready to be baptized.

For all of Augustine's powers of exposition, displayed in

page after page of his *Confessions,* he could not tell us exactly what happened to him that day in the garden. Somehow, in a matter of minutes, doubt turned to certainty, skepticism became faith. Upon the basis of his new faith, the master theologian would expound upon every major Christian idea—salvation, the Trinity, original sin, and the nature of the sacraments. Yet he could not explain the mystery of his own conversion or account for it except as in this brief description.

Isaac Newton's problem was a good deal simpler and less dramatic.

Like many stargazers and rock splitters before him, Sir Isaac had plunged into the mysteries of earthly and celestial mechanics. He was fascinated by the way the moon moves around the earth. He wondered why the moon in its comings and goings does not once in a while take a swipe at the earth, or go away for a week or two, or forever. Sir Isaac Newton was likewise curious about the free fall of objects, like the shot Galileo dropped from the tower of Pisa or bullets discharged from guns on the level. Galileo had *described* the movement of falling bodies very well; he had even figured out the formula of acceleration by which one can predict how fast a shoe will fall.

But no one, since Aristotle two thousand years before, had explained *why* things fall down, instead of up or sideways. Gravity was a mystery, pure and simple. Aristotle, in his best cracker-barrel manner, said that things fall to the earth because that is where they belong. Things like fire and smoke fly upward because they don't belong on the earth, but in Heaven. For Newton as for Galileo, this was an altogether unsatisfying response to the mystery. They might be amazed to hear that, as of 1988, Aristotle's homespun explanation serves as well as any.

But Newton wanted to know more about the ways of gravity, and so he thought, and he figured, and he speculated. One day, taking his leisure under an apple tree, and gazing up at the transparent moon whose attraction to the earth still mystified him, he was startled into awareness by an apple that knocked him on the head. He picked up the apple and looked at it. Then he looked at the moon and back at the apple.

Isaac Newton had had a mystical experience. It had dawned upon the scientist that gravity was not specific to the apple, the earth, or the moon. Gravity was a universal force of attraction between all things. He still did not know what it was. But he had been granted a mystical insight into the way gravity behaves. Twenty years would pass before he could explain what he had glimpsed in that thrilling moment under the apple tree. He would first have to invent a mathematical language to describe universal gravity—the integral calculus.

Now you may think, in the loftiness of modernity, that this discovery of Sir Isaac Newton's in 1675 was not such a big deal. You may think that Newton's insight seems not at all "mystical" in the sense of being remote from human understanding. But, remember, no one had ever dreamed of such a thing before 1675, *and nothing in the daily experience of our senses suggests* that there is a measurable attraction between, for instance, the coffee cup on your desk and the refrigerator. But there is.

I recall, from my high school physics class, the miraculous gyrations of the Cavendish balance. Inside a glass box a little steel shaft, with two spheres attached at each end, hangs horizontal, like a tiny barbell, from a thin thread tied at the middle. Outside the glass box on either side are two huge iron balls attached to a beam so they can rotate around the same axis as the tiny barbell under the glass.

I remember my physics teacher, who looked rather like a mad monk, proclaiming the law of universal gravitation to bored and skeptical students. Most of us were in love, or getting over it, or about to fall in love, and so we were hard pressed to concentrate on anything except for each other, as the bearded teacher swiveled the great beam of the Cavendish balance. But when I saw the little beam follow the great beam, and the tiny spheres irresistibly drawn to the heavy, I was thrilled. And I was as amazed as if my teacher had levitated, in a lotus position, above his cluttered desk.

When we had done pointing and shrieking, and demanded to know *why* these spheres were attracted to one another, the mad monk muttered something about Einstein and the curvature of the space-time continuum or some other such gibberish offensive to the critical intelligence of ninth-graders. And when we pursued him, he shrugged his shoulders, confessing he did not know, that Newton and Einstein had not figured it out, and probably nobody alive knew. It was a mystery.

So Newton's mystical experience enabled him to describe the mystery of gravity more effectively than his ancestors, and more usefully to be sure. All of later physics rests upon Newton's writings, just as Christian theology has its roots in Saint Augustine. But gravity, the thing itself, remains as much a mystery as the Holy Ghost. That so many people think of Saint Augustine as a mystic, and of Sir Isaac Newton as a scientist, reveals more about their religious opinions than about the adventures of mysticism or the consolations of science.

Love, like gravity, is a mystery. All discussions of love are more or less mystical when they are not descriptive. Though nobody can say exactly what love is, we have all seen the force in action and felt its movement. Any book that advertised itself as a "scientific" discussion of love would have to be dismissed as a fraud or suffered as a tastelessly prolonged joke. Love has a sense of humor, but the joke is on us if we do not recognize its ultimate seriousness.

Before I leave Sir Isaac Newton and the handy comparison of love and gravity, I ought to say that love, like gravity, answers to complex principles or laws. And the fact of love is so essential to our lives that to reject its principles would destroy the civilization that has been built upon it. Without the principle of general gravity, we would not have developed the sophisticated technology to put a satellite in orbit; without the principles of love in the Western world, we would have neither the Ten Commandments nor a cooperative democracy.

So, on the one hand, we have the mystery of love: dark, unfathomable, the subject of mystical speculations. And on the other hand, we have the laws, the reputed doctrine of love, what it must do and how it works. Love's doctrine as it has evolved in the Western world over the past several millennia appears to be as well defined and self-evident as the mystery is full of shadows and bewildering. What could be the purpose of any discussion, if love is either obvious, or utterly incomprehensible?

To be worthy of the subject, any conversation about love must honor the mystery by being bold to speculate upon it; to be useful, any discussion of love must criticize and bring the doctrine up to date, preparing for love the forms adequate to the world we are entering, the world of the 1990s.

History has piled up a sizable library of books about love and its symptoms, dating back to Plato's *Symposium*, which was written in the fourth century B.C. There is a great stack of books behind me in my studio: The most enduring and influential contributions to the doctrine of love, like the *Symposium*, and Saint Augustine's *Confessions*, the novels of Colette and the diaries of Anaïs Nin, are nakedly personal. The reason for this is evident. Those who take love seriously will entrust love's language and doctrine only to somebody deeply familiar with love's ways. They demand personal testimony as proof.

Now I am not about to write my autobiography at the tender age of forty. I do not yet know enough about my life.

One of the greatest books ever written on the subject of love, Stendhal's *De l'amour*, falters here and there as we suspect the writer may be unfit for certain kinds of love. But the great strength of his classic Romantic testament is its intimacy, a passionate love for the *reader*. The author who pretends to remain aloof from his subject or his readers by treating love clinically or scientifically, cannot hope to win people's trust for longer than the fashion of a season.

So I will not remain aloof. Upon the shaky premise that I can talk about love today with as much authority as I ever will, I shall offer my own stories by way of illustration, as if I were a Cavendish balance, turning its spheres now toward the greater spheres of filial love, or sibling or erotic love. My experience is limited, to be sure, so I will not pretend I have said all that should be said about love; my friends and family might be surprised that I fall so short even in my accounts of my own experience. But this is not an autobiography; it is a book about love, and such narrative as the book includes comes to light only in illustration of patterns I believe are common, though by no means universal. So you will always know what I am talking about when I refer to friendship or erotic love, parental or religious love. You may be sure I am talking about this friend I have introduced, or a particular sexual experience, or one of my own beliefs.

One of my beliefs is in love's power as a civilizing influence; another is that love is a great teacher, not only of civilizations but of individuals.

We learn from love, from the experiences of brotherhood, friendship, parenthood, from falling in and out of love, and in our pursuit of spiritual love. How often have we heard it said that "Mr. Smith has fallen in love, and how it has changed him!" Dour, humorless Mr. Smith, the auditor, who never had a smile or a good word for anyone, suddenly has a flower in his lapel and has been heard singing to himself in the corridor. Mr. Smith looks like the stock character in a situation comedy, Ebenezer Scrooge on Christmas day, yet he is drawn directly from life. And so what if Mr. Smith fails in pursuit of his lady, and next week resumes his dour mask and his most unmusical demeanor? He has been in love and learned from it certain possibilities of happiness. Mr. Smith will never be the same.

Once in a great while, every few hundred years or so, an entire civilization adapts to a new mode of love. Nations that have experienced a major redefinition of love's doctrine, can never be the same. Looking over my shoulder at the shelf of books that includes the *Symposium* and Saint Augustine's *Confessions* and D. H. Lawrence's *Sons and Lovers,* I can see the history of Western civilization as a series of profound, mass love affairs, in which an entire culture has fallen in love in a new way, with a different form of love. The form suits the time and place and moves the culture along to a higher stage of evolution. Likewise, as I look back over my own life, I can see in it a process of learning, or being led by, different forms of love—filial, fraternal, erotic. I notice a striking resemblance between the progress of my own education and the progress of love through history, from the wilderness of senses to the civilization of mind and spirit.

This moment is the perfect occasion to explore the mystery of love unfolding right here in our lives toward the end of the twentieth century. Many of us can see the parallel between personal experiences of love and the unfolding of the doctrine in history. Any one of us might make such a book. We may have been falling in love in the same way at the same time, our generation mirroring in one lifetime a historical process that has taken thousands of years.

Journalists and historians remind us, over and over, that the generation of Americans born in the 1940s (and a few years before and after) is weirdly special. Sometimes I think we are a whole history of civilization in microcosm, with agonizing responsibilities, including the survival of the human species.

I have no more reason to believe this than Isaac Newton had to believe in a universal force of gravity, and no less reason than Saint Augustine, who would live to summarize his beliefs in the remarkable phrase *Amor meus pondus meum,* or "Love is my weight."

If he had had the benefit of Sir Isaac Newton's mystical insight, Saint Augustine might have said, "Love is my gravity."

one

FILIAL LOVE

We are born from total darkness into a blinding light in which we cannot distinguish ourselves from mother or anything else in nature. Yet even before we recognize ourselves or our surroundings, love has been working on us for some time.

The first experience of love is of being loved, by our parents. We know our mother's affection before we can begin to understand it, and mirror love unconsciously. Years pass before sons and daughters comprehend the love that is their birthright—years, if not decades. In fact, I didn't understand very much about my parents' feelings until I had my own children, and then I was surprised by the magnitude of my emotion as the family circle was completed. By then, several varieties of love had inspired and tempered me; now all of these feelings harmonize in the passion I feel for my children, who seem to enlarge my emotional boundaries, and to promise a life after death.

But the first experience of *loving* is in loving our parents. Because filial love begins before we have language to define it, this first active love, so important in our lives, remains largely unexplained, undocumented.

Infants, of course, do not keep diaries or write letters. The most articulate four-year-old is more likely to be found composing a piano sonata or mastering the calculus than to be seen writing a book about love. By the time one has the skill and the desire to articulate such emotions, the memories of earliest childhood have dwindled. And the rough character of those feelings so challenges our sense of propriety and our peace of mind that the memory flatly refuses to cooperate. Memory folds its arms and informs us that the person we seek no longer lives there.

Many authors of autobiography, like Jean-Jacques Rousseau, will admit to no recollection of childhood before the age of five. Others record a few impressions but do not trust their memories to deliver an accurate account of infancy. I am blessed, or cursed, with a vivid memory of my childhood years beginning just before the age of three. I shall do my best to recall what I felt for my mother and my father, sparing no details that might illuminate the nature of filial love.

MY MOTHER

My mother, left alone for days at a time in a strange city, in a three-room apartment with no one to talk to but her baby, talked to the baby all day, as if he had full command of the King's English. My mother spoke beautifully and copiously, with a gentle southern accent.

By the age of two the baby had, according to my mother and other witnesses, if not full command of the language, at least the verbal authority of a lieutenant. Perhaps the early acquisition of language has given my memory a slightly longer reach than most people's. Most adults admit they can recall hardly a scene or event that occurred before the age of five. Doctor Freud might tell us that what happened in that prelinguistic era was so dreadful we are better off forgetting it, and so we do. But I have not forgotten. I remember very well what I felt for my mother and father between the ages of two and five.

We moved out of the three-room apartment in the summer of 1952, with months to prepare for my fourth birthday in October. This was celebrated with unforgettable fanfare in our new house. The moving date is significant in the architecture of my memory. It assures me that everything I remember happening in that small apartment transpired before I was three and a half years old. And I remember a lot, more than anyone would ever bother to tell me, and more than enough to have shocked my family with evidence they had hoped was buried forever.

The earliest memory I can document is the scene in the apartment the night my mother brought my newborn sister home from the hospital. She was born on May 5, 1950. I was exactly two and a half years of age. My grandmother and grandfather had driven to Washington from the Eastern Shore, to examine the new descendent and lend my mother a hand. If I cannot recall what the family wore that night, I do remember where they sat, the patterns of the carpet and the upholstery, and an atmosphere of joy mixed with anxiety. My grandparents were infrequent visitors in our home. Though they were broadminded people by any standards, they had expected something far different for their daughter than what my father had to offer.

That scene is the first I can nail to the calendar. Surely a number of my impressions predate that evening. Our second-story apartment opened, from the second landing of the interior stairwell, onto an L-shaped living and dining area. A large window in the living room looked west toward the avenue; and just around the corner in the dining room, another window looked south over the courtyard. So if you walked in the door on a bright day when the curtains were open, you could see through the living room into the dining-room window across the angle, and beyond the dining room, the door to a tiny kitchen. Straight back through the living room, a short hallway led to the bedrooms, my parents' room on the right and mine on the left next to the dining area. Not much could go on in this flimsily partitioned dwelling without everyone knowing about it.

The apartment was simply furnished, as suited my mother's taste and my father's means. An overstuffed sofa, long enough for a tall man to sleep on, ran the length of the wall across from the living-room window. On the adjacent wall, across from the entrance, was a mahogany desk whose drawers were off-limits because my father at night emptied his pockets into them. One morning I peeked into the top drawer, and saw money and keys and shiny copper cylinders with dark points. I ran to my mother holding one of the mysterious gems in my hand, and she told me it was a bullet. The sound on my mother's lips sounded frighteningly percussive. And I was never, never to go peeking into the desk drawer again.

On the floor was a worn Belgian carpet of black and red, which I got to know as only a child can know a carpet. The carpet did not follow us to the new house, but I remember its colors very well under the rungs and rockers of the wooden rocking chair which sat in the light of the living-room window.

My mother and I shared the daylight in the living room, as she rocked in that bentwood chair upon the seat of woven rushes and I moved in and out of her arms. My mother was a confirmed and zealous rocker, having been expertly rocked in her own infancy by my grandmother, who came from a long line of legendary rockers. She believed that it steadied the blood and defined the center of gravity in mother as well as child.

My mother has always had an enormous amount of nervous energy. So her attachment to the rocking chair should not be viewed as a symptom of laziness. Though she has since assured me she was blissfully happy in the years of early motherhood, sitting still was never her favorite part of the job description. Rocking is a way of sitting without sitting still. So she rocked, and I rocked right along with her. She rocked and she talked. And she sang in a clear, rich soprano voice.

My mother was, and is to this day, a strikingly beautiful woman. Now you may think I am saying this just because she is my mother and has shaped my conception of beauty. There is some truth in that. But it is also true that if you ask anyone else who has ever seen her, what does the woman look like? they may begin by telling you she is beautiful before they are pressed for details. A standing joke, when both women were a good deal younger, was that Elizabeth Taylor was the poor folks' imitation of my mother. And, indeed, a display of the photographs shows a remarkable similarity between the movie star and my mother, though my mother is fairer, with gray eyes and chestnut hair. My mother's chin is not so pointed as Elizabeth's. And then, a slight imperfection would save my mother from the perils of professional beauty: her eyes are a trifle too close together, a feature I have come to associate with intellectual concentration.

My mother's looks never seemed to be a burden to her. She had a fortunate sense of humor about her beauty which sometimes verged on self-deprecation. She tells me her mother had a hand in this, discouraging any delight in physical endowments as "vanity," while insisting upon more durable virtues. So my mother was also kind, and warmhearted, and charitable to family, friends, and strangers.

If this begins to sound like a Hallmark celebration of my mother, then for the moment it must. If I should tell you I

love my mother, what could this possibly mean to you if you
do not understand her perfections? My mother has her share
of imperfections, and I may have occasion to mention those,
too. But her faults are not the sort that would be troubling,
or even noticeable, to a child of five, any more than they
would be harmful to an infant. So far as I knew then, she was
perfect.

So we sat, in the sunlight, rocking. I can recall with
exquisite vividness my mother's face, musing or smiling, the
firmness of her hands lifting me in and out of her lap, and
the warmth of her body under a blue apron, moving back and
forth in the chair. Waking and sleeping, we were like a single
body, utterly content. I went to sleep in her arms and would
awaken there. When I wanted to get down and crawl or walk,
she would put me down, and I would play on the rug in the
warm circumference of her vision, which seemed to me as
vital as her touch, a smooth transition from physical contact
to an invisible bond that permitted freedom without fear. To
hear her tell it, the parturition had been just as smooth, an
easy delivery.

As long as we were touching, I did not need to see her.
When I got down from her lap and let go of her hand, then
I needed to see her, constantly at first, then intermittently
like friends parting at a station. I would look back quickly,
to make sure she was still there, smiling. I was accustomed
to what seemed perpetual contact with her in my waking
moments, physical contact as proof of her existence; so it
would take me a while before I could believe the evidence of
my eyes: she was still there.

And not until her face was exactly painted upon the canvas
of my imagination, could I trust my mother for long enough
that I might wander off out of sight, into the dining room,
under the stainless steel and Formica-top table. At that turning
point, which must have come before my second birthday, the
love that Rousseau calls sensual, instinctive love matured into

a full-blown sentiment, the love that would be the spring of all other passions.

Away from my mother for a few moments, exploring a pattern in the carpet, I would remember suddenly, joyfully, that she was still in the next room. I would long to be with her. If she was where I left her, reading a book, I was delighted. If she was not there in the rocking chair when I returned, I was at first angry. And then I would get scared. And if the front door should be open . . .

How long does it take a child to love the mother with a sentiment that transcends physical instinct? Exactly as long as it takes the child to develop the faculty of imagination. The image enables us to believe that moment follows moment: Mother's life will continue even if you turn your back on her for a while. Mother's image in the child's mind makes this possible. Before that, the relationship is still symbiotic; there is no real differentiation of the parts, mother and child. Once the child has developed an imagination, he becomes sufficiently aware of parting and reunion that he can experience filial love.

This is the age that children, the world over, love to play peek-a-boo. Now you see me, now you don't. Playing peek-a-boo with Mama is a game with high stakes at the outset, and high drama. There's Mama, smiling over the rail of the crib. Suddenly she's gone. The baby is puzzled at first. Where's Mama? Then the baby gets worried, the little brow furrows. Mama's gone. Is she gone forever? Mama's image pops into the baby's mind to take the edge off the anxiety. The baby knows Mama lives and wants her to come back. Peek-a-boo! There's Mama again, smiling over the side of the crib! The baby squeals with delight.

If the baby's imagination is sufficiently tuned, the game is endless fun, a tragedy with a happy ending, more hilarious each time you play it. But if the child is too young, the game is not the least bit funny, because the child may think his mother will never return.

There is a cruel variation of peek-a-boo, less often played because children enjoy it less. If they are under the age of three, they will probably dislike it. Mama or Papa, in plain sight, calls the child's name. The child answers, "Here I am!" But the parent pretends not to hear or see the child, and goes on looking, under the furniture, behind the curtains, calling the child's name urgently while the child answers, "Here I am!" and tries to make contact with the dodging parent.

I have seen children driven to the edge of hysteria by this game before the parent finally faces the child, and *notices* him, and says with a great sigh of relief, "Oh, *there* you are!" At which point the child laughs, relieved of a burden far heavier than any placed upon him by peek-a-boo.

This game is terrifying to the child, as a premonition of death. Invisible to his mother, the child has become a ghost. To enjoy peek-a-boo the baby needs only a sharp enough image of Mama to guarantee she endures in absence, and therefore will return. But to be brave in "Here I am," the little person must believe in his *own* existence, apart from anybody else's testimony. The child must have developed a strong *self*-image in order not to be thrown into a panic by such a game.

My mother's games were always kind, and I trusted her completely. She was everything that was good, and just, and pleasant, despite her handling of my Pablum spoon, which I endured in silent annoyance.

Fifteen years later, apropos of nothing, I looked up from my reading and called to my mother. She was setting the table in the dining room when I startled her with the prehistoric complaint. I cried out that, in feeding me Pablum, she would shovel in a load with the spoon on the level, which was fine; but then she would yank the spoon shaft skyward toward my nose so that the spoon wrenched my upper palate, which was not fine at all. It was a nuisance. My mother, as if the alleged offense had occurred last week, explained that she was merely trying to keep the food in my mouth. She told me that all mothers do the same, and no baby had ever been so ungrateful as to complain about it. And that I ought to put the book down and help her set the table. I did that.

I mention the offense of the spoon because this was exceptional, outstanding in my memory because my mother seemed to me, in those years, to be perfect in everything. Naturally I wanted to do all I could to please her. She was easy to please in physical ways—I was agreeably affectionate, had a good appetite, and was digestively regular in all those ways that so please mothers—and she was generous in praising my humblest contributions. But she made me so happy I wanted to do something more for her. I did not realize what it was until I got out into the open air and on my own.

This may seem strange to suburban parents of the late twentieth century, who have cause to fear for their children's safety until the children are old enough to defend themselves. But from the time I was big enough to venture out the door, I was given the run of the three-building apartment complex—the laundry room, the front lawn that sloped down to the highway, and the playgrounds and fenced gardens behind the buildings.

My mother had grown up in a small country town where everybody knew the children, so they were always within earshot of someone who cared about them. She had no reason to believe the new suburbs of Washington, D.C., would be any different, and quickly made friends with her neighbors. I was tall for my age and full of energy and curiosity, so when I wanted out, she opened the door and let me go.

I played in the flowering hedges under our windows. I ran around the brick walls of our apartment building to the lawn in back. From time to time, the image of my mother's face would appear to superimpose itself upon the landscape as a pleasant reassurance that she was still at home and would be there when I got back.

On a little hill in view of the rear windows of our apartment, I noticed a few dandelions and violets growing. These were the most pleasing things in sight. I thought of my mother, smiling. I pulled the violets and dandelions out of the grass and hurried home to give the flowers to my mother. I thought that this would be the very thing to please her beyond anything I had ever done before, and it was. However happy she may have been to see me return, she was even happier when she received the violets and dandelions. Later that night I could not sleep for the bitter taste in my mouth that had come with the milk of the dandelions, but that bitterness became part of the strength of the memory.

That is my earliest distinct memory of being outdoors by myself. Like other scenes from the same period, this is impossible to date exactly. But I am sure I must have been younger than three years of age. The memory is significant in this context because it clearly connects my feeling for my mother with my feeling for the natural world of flowers, grass, and sunlight; it is perhaps equally significant in proving that my part in the parent-child relationship was not then wholly passive. At three years of age, I had a distinct sense that I was producing love by my own activity.

All my recollections here are tinged with nostalgia. But this is the nostalgia proper to and inseparable from love, rather than any excess of purple sentiment. I do not have any paradisal memory of life in the womb, and I am skeptical of people who claim to recall prebirth experiences under hypnosis. Yet I was surely affected by those easy months in my mother's belly, as I am certain she was changed by my presence there.

Early childhood, as I remember those years in the company of my mother, was indeed a kind of paradise in which even the process of teething could be endured with equanimity. If

I was happier before, I cannot remember or imagine it. I have been as happy since, but only for hours at a time.

THE NOBLE SAVAGE

My earliest memories of my father are of a man asleep, sometimes in my mother's bed and sometimes on the couch in the living room.

He was long and had wiry black hair that sprung wild on the pillow, and a dark shadow of beard on his face. But he looked harmless enough, like pretty much any other man asleep. My mother would put her finger to her lips, telling me to go softly so as not to wake him. I must play quietly so as not to rouse him, because he had come in very late at night.

Often my mother and I would get dressed and tiptoe out the door, so I could run and shout in the open air of the playground.

Or she would buckle me into the stroller and push me along the elm-lined paths of the Resurrection Fathers' splendid estate on the hill. This mysterious order of Catholic priests lived in seclusion in a Victorian mansion overlooking our apartment. There I could whoop it up on the lawn, out of earshot of my sleeping father.

He was then twenty-one years old, a couple of years younger than my mother. He stood six feet tall, with the physique, as well as the temperament, of a light-heavyweight prize-fighter.

My mother had thought she was the younger of them until the afternoon they applied for a marriage license. They had eloped that morning, against everyone's wishes and advice. He would always insist my mother had been the chief instigator of the abduction, that she had robbed the cradle, an accusation my mother will not deny or confirm.

Anyway he drove his convertible coupe nonstop from her

little hometown on the Eastern Shore of Maryland to the busy metropolis of Washington, D.C. They arrived at his family's place of business, a shooting-gallery amusement arcade on wicked Ninth Street. My father had to get some sort of note from his father to give to the justice of the peace so that the young couple could get married. My father was underage.

Theirs had been a whirlwind courtship, and such details as age and religion seemed unimportant. My mother was adventurous and liked surprises—this would be the first of many in her new life. Actually, my father's age was even less meaningful than my mother knew at the time, because he lived by a calendar that bore no relation to anyone else's. Years would go by before she could understand this. Finding out how young her fiancé actually was, my mother was startled, not so much that she had been wooed under a false pretense (had she ever *asked* him his age?), but that the boy seemed so old. At nineteen he looked and acted like a thirty-year-old man. And he owned his own business, and a Cadillac, and dental plates. She had been intrigued by him before; now she was downright awestruck. What on earth had the boy been doing that aged him so quickly?

The dreadful circumstances of my father's childhood forced him to blossom out of season like a jungle plant, absurdly, wildly, incredibly. Soon after he was born, his parents were divorced—remarkable for a Jewish couple in the 1920s. His mother, never too stable emotionally, was so undone by the breakup of her marriage that she neglected to care for my father, who became the unwanted charge of the extended family.

From all accounts, the day he was on his feet my father was out the door, and whoever intended to take care of him would have to catch him first. One of his aunts tells the story of my father in a cowboy hat, at the age of three, running into a saloon on Ninth Street, a block ahead of the babysitters.

There he barricaded himself behind the bar from where he could pelt the posse with lemons and pickled eggs. Inspired by movies of the cowboy Hoot Gibson, the three-year-old desperado would make his escape through the rear exit. Armed with two seltzer bottles, one in each hand, he fired salvos of seltzer water into the eyes of his pursuers, as he backed into the arms of a policeman in the alley.

One aunt after another tried and failed to take care of my father. Later they would proudly display their scars to prove it. Some time after his standoff at the saloon, my father's innate curiosity, unsupervised, led him to pry the cap off a steam radiator. For weeks he lay in a hospital bed, near death from the scalding, his body robbed of phosphorus and calcium so his teeth would never grow, and his abdomen so hideously scarred that he would forever wear his belt buckle on his hip to avoid the pain.

Not long after he got out of the hospital, my father disappeared. He was four. The police eventually found him on old Route 1, midway between Washington and Baltimore, pedaling away furiously on his bicycle, still pedaling as they lifted him *off* the bicycle and hustled him into the squad car. He was headed north to visit his Uncle Henry, a good-humored and kindly gangster who had taken a special interest in the high-spirited child.

School for him was impossible, or nearly impossible. If he had not been so intelligent, nothing on earth could have kept him in the classroom. And he was sociable, and his friends were in school. Teachers were awed at his quickness, particularly with numbers, and there was enough excitement in the books and lessons to engage his curiosity and keep him coming back for more, at least for a few years.

I have tried and failed to find any record of where he lived during the seven years he attended school. Neither my father nor anyone else could remember. You ordinarily think of children as living in a house, or apartment, and sleeping in their own bedroom. Not my poor father. We know of various homes where he slept; but he seems literally to have lived on the streets of Northwest Washington, D.C., and slept in the home of whatever friend or relative happened to be nearest at the hour when he could no longer keep his eyes open.

He was learning his trade as a mechanic. At the age of seven or eight, my father showed a knack for fixing machinery. He loved to fix things and learned quickly who would pay him for his skill. Pinball machines came into vogue in the 1930s. The pinball machine, celebrating technology's coming of age, technology's service of individual fantasy, became a gold mine in the Depression years. A good-natured Greek entrepreneur, Nick Gazoulas, who owned a route of pinball machines in Washington, D.C., let my father sleep under one of the machines after the boy had fixed it for him. Nick the Greek was willing to pay good money to keep his pin-games ringing and flashing, and the little Jewish boy was a prodigy at this. After the amusement arcades were closed, he worked long into the night fixing machines.

By the time my father was thirteen, his income was in five figures, and his schedule did not mesh with the schedule of classes at Mount Rainier High School. So he quit school. And he set up housekeeping in bachelor's quarters at the Hotel Houston in downtown Washington.

The day he met my mother on the Eastern Shore in 1947, my father was eighteen years old and had been living in bachelor's quarters for five years. He had been through two or three luxury motorcars and at least twice as many affairs of the heart. He had dined upon the best cuisine the restaurants of Baltimore, Washington, and New York could provide him; he had become a master horseman and assembled a wardrobe of flashy high-fashion clothing that rivaled Sinatra's. During the war (in which he had been too young to serve, as well as disinclined) vending operators were flying the "whiz kid" from coast to coast to work on various kinds of amusement machinery, from slot machines and peepshow panorams to Ferris wheels and roller coasters. In 1947 he was the manager of Glen Echo Amusement Park; with that salaried position, plus his income as a free-lance mechanic, the eighteen-year-old was making about thirty thousand dollars a year, in an era when that was serious money.

My mother was meeting an eighteen-year-old boy with the life experience of a thirty-year-old man who had been robbed of his childhood.

At that point, my father had all the verbal skills of a Hottentot, a noble savage who stammered pathetically. He had not learned the beauties of language at his mother's knee, nor in the street gangs, nor in the long hours after midnight as he sat alone deciphering the complex wiring codes of pinball machines in the days before printed circuits. The boy had never finished a book. And now he had to face my mother, who had read her way through the entire library of Vienna, Maryland.

It was not an intellectual affinity that drew my parents together, but raw desire. I can imagine the two of them, gorgeous savages, communicating their most urgent and complex needs and states of mind with grunts, rolling eyes, and wild gestures, like barbarians, mating without benefit of tribal rituals. I can imagine my father clubbing my mother on the head and dragging her away, or vice versa.

Yet there must have been tenderness, at the beginning. The two of them were romantic in the rather moony, dewy-eyed style of the 1940s. And certainly they were as thoroughly in love as any two people have ever fallen upon such short notice. The whole courtship, from introduction to vows, did not take up more than a few weeks of their time. Both of them had fine singing voices, and my father particularly loved to sing because while singing he did not stammer. And so he learned the lyrics of all the popular love ballads and, with his eyes half-closed, crooned them to my mother in the autumn moonlight. The two lovers did not need to speak a word if they did not wish to.

My mother's mother, an upright Episcopal lady for all her humble circumstances, was horrified that her daughter might marry this big-city Jew who arrived in the tiny town in a huge car with a musical horn, and fretted over it terribly. My mother, a good-hearted girl, did not keep my grandmother in suspense. She ran off and married the swarthy Jew only a few weeks after being cautioned against it, and then she went to spend her life with him in the distant city.

They were married by a justice of the peace in October, and I was born exactly a year later.

Of all the characters recent civilization has produced, or suffered to flourish, my father comes the closest to realizing Rousseau's ideal of the Noble Savage.

Nobody ever told him what to do or what he should not do, and his hard-earned morality must have taxed him. He did not grow up in a home with parents to provide the examples of fatherhood and motherhood that serve most of us in our own experiments as parents, husbands, or wives. But he fell in love, and at eighteen woke up one morning to find himself married. At nineteen he rubbed his eyes and saw that he had fathered a son. Now this man who had never listened to anyone tell him what to do, suddenly had a wife and a little boy and an apartment where he was expected to return every night.

What was he supposed to do?

He made it up as he went along. With absolutely no help from role models, books, or psychotherapists, my father invented a plan of how the family should operate, and everyone's proper role in the organization, as if he had been chief architect of the family structure before the Flood. His sense of family was based upon his understanding of the individual in the society where he had grown up. He might have said, if he had had the language to express it: *The family should be a unit for defense in a great war, where one survives by virtue of cunning and courage and unwavering family loyalty.*

His job was to provide for us. So he worked long hours, as manager of Glen Echo Amusement Park and as a free-lance mechanic. Soon after marriage he assumed an enormous debt his father owed the federal government for back taxes. So my father was suddenly poor and had to work harder than ever. Like many vending-machine mechanics, he made big money late at night in overtime, when traffic is slow and the machines can be shut down and repaired without disrupting business. He got home at three o'clock in the morning, and it was my mother's job to feed him.

He was an all-powerful tyrant. If he had not loved us so much, our life with him would have been intolerable.

My mother was learning to cook. If my father did not approve of a recipe, he would throw the saucepan containing the offending substance clattering against the wall, and my mother would prepare something else. Words could not express his outrage. He was hungry, and he was tired. I may have been awakened once or twice by the sound of pans and dishes crashing against the wall between the dining area and my bedroom, or it may have been thunder. I do remember seeing colorful collages of eggs and catsup and mashed potatoes on the walls as my mother and I tiptoed past my sleeping father on the way outside to play.

My father was weary from working and creating his entire character and morality out of whole cloth with nobody to help him, in a more or less brutal marketplace. He was furious. This is the word that best describes him in those years, and my mother and I naturally believed that we were to blame for his anger, that he was furious with us for something we had done or failed to do. In fact, one of the chief reasons he was furious was because he could not speak. He was bursting with ideas, questions, and whole theories about life and the cosmos; and he had no better means of expressing himself than cursing or throwing a pot against the wall. Eventually he would develop a marvelous sense of humor, and skills as a teacher and raconteur. But even the sense of humor would remain latent until he learned to speak, which would not happen for another decade, when wealth suddenly thrust him into a new social stratum.

Naturally, my earliest memory of my father is that I was terrified of him. Like a thunderbolt the man divided the perfect solitude of that paradise my mother and I enjoyed. When he awakened, in the early afternoon, he was hungry again and had to be fed immediately. It was my mother's job to cook the dinner, and mine to come to the table when called, conduct myself properly, and eat all of the food on my plate.

My father looked angry, his dark eyes staring intently at the middle of the table, at nothing. He looked like a man who wanted desperately to say something but could not find the words. We wanted to please him, to smooth the furrow from his brow any way we could.

My mother would ask him if the food was tasty. The food was fine. What was he thinking? He told me to finish my string beans. I had tried and tried. He told me again, in a loud, stern voice. He had told me over and over that I could never leave the dinner table until I had finished all the food on my plate. I tried again, and this time the food stuck in my throat and I gagged. My father shouted at me not to do that. He told my mother that I was not to leave the table until I had eaten all of the food. And then, to my great relief, he walked out of the room.

I sat in front of the cold food. Twilight came and went, and the room filled with shadows. I fell asleep with my face in the uneaten food, which my father insisted be served up to me the next evening, and so on, until it had been eaten, either by me or the roaches, whoever got to it first.

That is my first clear memory of a dramatic situation involving my father. And I believe his punitive role is significant to the larger discussion of filial love. I wished to please my father, as my mother did, and neither of us had the slightest idea how to go about it. What I soon learned was how to *displease* him, for he was quick to show his displeasure and punish me in a way I would not soon forget. None of this was casual, capricious, or intentionally cruel on my father's part. Like everything else he would ever have to do with me, the punishments were carefully considered for my benefit: if I was not to grow up a coddled ignoramus, I must learn there would be painful consequences for bad behavior.

Like ideologues the world over, my father lacked a sense of proportion. For minor offenses like speaking out of turn, he would ask me to stand in the corner. Given my precocious vocabulary in the face of his poor, stammering speech, perhaps my interrupting him was not so minor an offense. But he would send me to the corner of the dining room and force me to stand there with my back to the company for what seemed like an eternity to a three-year-old. My mother now says that those confinements were cruelly long, sometimes more than an hour, and he would not accept her pleas for my release. Now I think my powers of concentration, in solitude, may have originated there, in being forced into corners at such a tender age. Yet I would not recommend the program for any other child.

For more serious crimes like drawing on the walls, stealing, or throwing rocks at automobiles or neighbor's windows, I had to face corporal punishment, as did many children of my generation and earlier. This custom has declined in recent years, probably for the best. Punitive measures are gradually giving way in child rearing to "positive reinforcement," which seems much more civilized and humane for parents and children alike.

But my father's way with "the strap" was old-fashioned and

instinctive, if not actually primitive. He hated it, and my mother says he returned from the sessions in tears, hoping each would be the last, that I would not prove as wild and unmanageable as he had been.

My memory of my father as high judge and executioner, and the way fear colored my love for him, typify an ancient and almost universal paradigm. Children perceive the father's love as conditional. Father will love me if I do the right thing, and he will not love me if I do the wrong thing. Mother will love me no matter what I do—she has no control over it. Mother and I are so much a part of each other that she must love me as a part of herself. Father is a part of the "other world." He will love me insofar as I abide by the rules of that world over which he is the ultimate judge.

I have gotten up these sketchy portraits of my father and mother not so much for their own interest as to serve the discussion. Without the least gesture toward tradition (apart from a courthouse marriage), these two renegades, my parents, reproduced an archetype so basic and primitive they might as well have been living in a cave as an apartment building. My mother stayed there with the baby and waited for her mate to return from fighting other cavemen for haunches of the buffalo. She was not stupid, or lazy, or backward. My mother had been to college, though it could not hold her interest, or her either, for more than a year. She had not been raised to be a fifth-century guardian of the hearth or a nursemaid. And my father was not bound by any orthodox code of male supremacy to keep wives indoors and children subservient. Yet my parents lived that way, right in the middle of the twentieth century, as if the wheel had yet to be invented.

My mother and I were at peace while we were alone, a perfect solitude *à deux* in the rocking chair by the window. I was afraid of my father because he disturbed the peace. In that way he was like many fathers the world over, from the beginning of time. Years later I would learn that he was a greater disturber of the peace and more frightening by far than other people's fathers, because of his extraordinary vigor and an intelligence that might never find its proper expression. When I had grown to appreciate his characteristics, then I could begin to understand why I felt about him the way I did.

I loved my father much as my mother did, with a certain intuitive sympathy for the good that was growing in him. He was not patient or entertaining when I was an infant. He did not get down on the floor and play with me. My father smiled now and then when I amused him and in moments of reflexive pride, but such moments were infrequent. I never knew what to do that would please him; I only knew from his melodramatic lessons when, and how, I had displeased him. He had a violent temper when he was a young man, and sometimes behaved horribly. Yet I sensed that my father was good. You cannot conceal this from a child.

We love people not because they are pleasant, well mannered, or well behaved. We love them for the good that is growing in them. If you are a saint, you may love the lowliest criminal or wastrel for the divinity that animates all human flesh; but most of us are not saints. We have normal capacities for love, and we love different people for their different virtues—one for physical beauty, one for humor, one for generosity. It did not take a saint to see the good in my father. I knew he was vastly intelligent, had physical appeal surpassing the average, and a great heart. He loved me and I knew it. You cannot deceive a child in this, though you may deceive yourself.

This brings us to the tragedy potential in parenting, and to a certain inequity between parent and child.

Some people do not love their fathers or mothers, and these children may be forgiven. But parents who do not love their children are never forgiven. Long after such parents expect to be safely dead, they will find themselves alive in the child's memory, where they are being roasted over a slow fire. There is no eleventh commandment saying that *thou shalt love thy children*; it is no more necessary than a commandment that *thou shalt eat and drink.* Those who do not love their children are cursed, because if you cannot love your children you cannot love at all. Fortunately this is as rare as to beget a daughter with six fingers on one hand, or one eye of blue and one of brown. My father loved me, as most fathers do; knowing that he loved me, I could tolerate practically any amount of bad behavior on his part and recover from it. If he had not loved me, he might have had the beautiful manners of the Duke of Windsor, and sat with me by the hour on the beach building sandcastles, yet none of the show would have mattered. As he did love me, I was content in his presence as long as I did not offend him.

I loved my father in admiration and wonder shot through with fear—not so much the fear that he would hurt me, though he seemed capable—rather the fear that I would do wrong and displease him, or that I might never be sufficiently good to avoid his displeasure.

Wherever I suspect my own experience departs from the base-lines of the human family—that is, the family experience as common to the suburban bourgeois, the Renaissance guild family, or the longshoreman's of the 1930s—I will red-letter our eccentricity or avoid using it as an illustration. I shall not refer to experiments in communal child raising or upper-class English households, in which children are raised by nannies and tutors.

Children of the present generation do not spend as much time in the company of their mothers as I did; many grow up in day-care centers and nurseries and in the care of baby-sitters, as more and more mothers enter the workforce. That was not the common experience of my generation of Americans, nor of humankind in general. Most of us grew up in close quarters with our fathers and mothers, or with surrogates of our parents; and insofar as love reveals itself in patterns, these may be perceived more readily in ordinary experience than in eccentricity.

That the father's love is conditional, and the mother's absolute, is one such pattern; the child's response to this predicament is my own unsurprising development of the general theorum. Erich Fromm, Jean-Jacques Rousseau, and other theorists put the burden of this dilemma upon the parents, suggesting that they are responsible for the child's feelings.

From all I know of our family home, my father's love was really no more conditional than my mother's; and yet I perceived it as conditional, because my father was large and frightening, and my mother was soft and comfortable.

I *saw* I was different from my mother, and felt the difference within. I saw I was more like my father; and from the moment I realized that, I longed to be like him and enter his world, to master the world outside as he had done. The fact that I began by being afraid of him was just one of the hurdles I would have to get over.

As soon as I was old enough to stay out from underfoot, he would take me with him, once in a while, to where he worked. I was about seven years old when he first let me go with him to the amusement arcade on Ninth Street, where he had taken over his father's failing business. The green neon sign in the window over the hot dog stand said "Playland." It was a wonderland for a boy, this cavernous nineteenth-century storefront, around the corner from the Capitol building, this circus smelling of hot dogs and onions and gunpowder, ringing with the sound of pinball machines and cash registers, the crack-crack of the shooting-gallery rifles and the clatter of peepshow projectors. In the rear of the building was a dark little office where my grandfather sat, a round, uncommunicative Jew with a mustache. He sat at a desk next to the huge gilded Mosler safe, counting the money.

This was my father's world, a kingdom in which he ruled supreme, with ritual deference to my grandfather. I was the crown prince. There is a theory that when private property came into being, and a man's son could inherit the property, the father began to look for the son best fitted to become his heir—the son most like him, the son he liked the best. I was built like my father, and looked enough like him that the employees loved to make a big fuss over the resemblance, calling me "the little boss."

As my father went on his rounds among the panorams and pinball games, and back and forth from the refreshment bar in the front of the arcade to the machine shop and the office in the back, I would tag along behind him, aping his stride. He had a pronounced swagger in those days, from side to side, up and down on his toes, his hands turned in and slightly extended from his hips, light-fisted, pugilistic. I mimicked him perfectly without realizing it, and everybody flattered us by noting the resemblance.

I would become as much like my father as I could, because I loved him and believed that to be like him was surely the straightest route to his approval. It seemed to me I was following him on the road of adventure into the world.

Language would become a point of conflict between us, as my verbal abilities far surpassed his, limiting my ability to identify with my father. But he never ridiculed my speech, as a more defensive, insecure man might have done. Instead, he improved his own. About the time of my bar mitzvah, my father learned to talk; and when he did, such a flood of language burst forth as has seldom been heard before or since, and we thought he might never stop talking.

But at first I worked very successfully at identifying with my father. The scar on his abdomen forced him to wear his belt buckle on his hip; I wore mine the same, imitating as style what I did not understand to be his shift against pain.

My sister, of course, had a different feeling for my father.

She looked even more like him than I did, with her black curly hair and dark eyes. Yet my impression is that she had no desire to be like my father, though she would recite, as I did, her part in little comedy routines that pleased him. My mother recalls that my sister would awaken in her crib no matter what hour my father came home at night, while I, a lighter sleeper, would never stir. My sister wanted to see him and hear his voice. My father was not very demonstrative in tender ways; the women of the family were grateful for whatever kind of attention he paid them. For my part, I did not care much what he did, as I said before, so long as I could be in his presence without riling him up. My love for him did not need any blandishments in order to flourish. He loved me, and he kept his promises, pleasant and unpleasant. I could be absolutely sure of him, and that is what mattered to me.

There is a difference between a son's love and a daughter's. I cannot speak confidently for women, I can only echo what I have heard. I have heard that the lucky daughters of affectionate men know a sweetness of love for father no boy can quite feel—and this feeling of perfect filial harmony is one the daughter cannot feel for mother.

Over the years we changed, my father, my mother, my sister, and I. My mother grew more confident of herself, and forceful in her resistance to my father's control. My father became a little more gentle and communicative with all of us. I grew to understand my own value as an individual, in a typical pattern of growth that effects the only notable change in the relations between a child and his parents: I became an emotional equal. Thus we came to a deeper understanding of our feelings for one another year by year; and this understanding may have enriched our emotions.

Yet the quality of the love did not change. You cannot make a rose of a cabbage, or alter the chemistry of love once it has fully bonded two people, though you may improve your understanding of it. As I got older I became more conscious of my feelings, but the basic emotion of filial love did not change after childhood. My love for my father remains tinged with the fear I will never quite manage to please him. And my love for my mother has never lost its confidence, or a certain sadness of nostalgia for a former paradise whose bliss can never be recaptured.

two

SIBLING LOVE AND

CHILDHOOD FRIENDSHIP

MY SISTER

I have one sister with unmistakable virtues and minor failings, and I was expected to love her. I do love her, with a bittersweet passion that must flavor sibling love as the rule rather than the exception.

My sister is brilliant, and a successful journalist. She so much resembles me physically it would seem like false modesty for me to say she is not quite attractive. I am larger than most grown men, and she is bigger than I. She has read *Finnegan's Wake* by James Joyce, a book I cannot open without suffering vertigo.

My sister can wear the clothes of an Irish fisherman, and address everyone, from street sweepers to titled nobility, as if she had made mudpies and blown bubbles with them. She does not have the mild, featureless character that one might love without thinking about it.

Headstrong, opinionated, outspoken, she is not a person I would seek out for a friend, for all her unmistakable virtues. She can be melancholy. With her dark hair and heavy black eyebrows, she broods. Against the injustices and madness of the world she sometimes rails, heroically, like Lear. Her best friends forgive this in her, for she has a sense of humor that can light up the darkness, and is generous in using that humor to comfort friends in need.

Had I been lucky enough to have five brothers and sisters, maybe I might love one of them as I love my best friend or my wife. But this seems to defy the law of averages. After all, I have chosen my best friends, and they have chosen me, from a cast of thousands.

Sentimentalists sing the praises of the family home, insisting that brothers and sisters who share the home and hearth, breathing the same air, eating at the same table, must be bound together forever by affection for their common past. I do not believe it. The truth is, the shared environment and heredity are likely to breed brothers and sisters with common values to unite them; but when the siblings' values or temperaments clash, as they often do, no amount of nostalgia for the ancestral home is likely to reconcile the siblings in unalloyed love.

I remember, just dimly, my mother being pregnant with my sister. As my mother grew larger and larger with the baby inside of her, I had the sense that this baby we were expecting was a part of my mother's body.

I distinctly remember the night my mother came home from the hospital and my grandparents came to visit. And I recall my relief and happiness when my mother came home, because I was not accustomed to being separated from her. My mother looked weary, holding the baby in her arms, for it had been a long and difficult labor.

My mother handed the slumbering newborn, smelling of talcum and oil, to my grandmother, and embraced me. My mother was not so big now as she had been before. Someone asked me to look at my new sister, and I did, as my grandmother leaned toward me so I could see into the bunting. I was curious, but not very curious. The sleeping baby seemed to me part of my mother still—somehow free-floating. Insofar as I can remember any feeling for my sister at that moment, I loved the infant as I loved my mother's hands and knees.

The baby slept in a crib in my room. I kept getting out of bed to look through the bars of the crib at my sleeping sister, more and more curious about her.

She was an altogether agreeable baby who ate and slept well, and smiled and chirped in the best baby fashion. I cannot remember any jealousy on my part, any feeling of invasion. There was plenty of room in my mother's life and heart for two children, and I was still so much a part of my mother I would have felt much the same as she did. I have asked her recently whether she can remember how I responded to the birth of my sister. My mother confirms I was enthusiastic about the adventure, especially the gadgetry that goes with caring for newborns: the convertible bassinet, the formula bottles, baby clothes and blankets and diapers and, of course, the toys. She tells me I was an adept and willing lieutenant in all baby maneuvers at home and in the field, including changing, feeding, and clothing my sister. And I knew exactly where the supplies and accessories were stored, from ointments to safety pins. When the babysitter came through the door, she was told to report to me for briefing and instructions.

My sister learned to talk before we moved out of the apartment. She was eleven months old. In our family we attach great significance to the first words the child says distinctly after it has learned to say "Mama" and "Papa." My sister's first words, spoken loud and clear when she and I were squeezed together on a bed next to my mother were: "Move over."

And move over I did.

My little sister and I got along beautifully, until she was old enough to get into my closet and cart my toys all over the house and into the yard. She dressed up in my cowboy suit and hat. She was a most cheerful, round-faced, and singing baby, with a head covered with black curls. My mother says my sister was truly an angel until she was four years old. At that point, she began to throw tantrums. She would scream so we feared her vocal cords would snap like rubber bands. She would stop her breath, she would roll on the floor and bite the furniture.

I tried everything I could think of to comfort her, bringing her toys, a stuffed bear or jack-in-the-box, reading a book or doing a dance I thought might divert her. But when I could not console my sister, I would tease her and torment her. I would tickle her, which made her hysterical, and invent silly names for her—*noodle, fingergush*—pronouncing her name backward or splicing it with an animal's, which she hated. Under the circumstances, my sister had no choice but to develop a marvelous sense of humor, which she did, and the ability to withdraw both physically and mentally from any company that did not quite suit her.

She had a miniature city of plastic houses and people and animals she ruled as mayor and deity, dispensing justice, life, joy, calamity, and death. Before she reached school age, my sister spent most of her time supervising the citizens of that imaginary country. She did not like to go outside and play, despite my mother's pleading. Before she got to school, her best friend in the world besides our mother was the teddy bear, Smokey, to whom she seemed attached like a Siamese twin.

She hated school. I remember taking my sister to school on the first day, and leaving her at the door of the classroom where she said goodbye to me, tearfully. All day I tried to keep an eye on her, looking into the window of her classroom, watching my sister on the playground at recess. In class she stayed in a corner by herself, and on the playground she wandered alone, her overcoat slung over her shoulder, like a convict doing time in a foreign prison.

Two years later, things were not much better, so my mother ordered a battery of psychological tests. They discovered that my sister was just fine except that she had an I.Q. of about 180. What in the world did she have to say to anyone under the age of twelve? There was talk of sending her to a special school for people who were intelligent, but my father would not hear of it.

My sister was one of those gifted children more comfortable with adults, for the most part, than with people her own age. She talked to adults, her aunts and uncles, and door-to-door salesmen. She talked to Leonard Eisenberg's father, Mel, who lived down the street. Mel was a good-natured, handsome Jewish merchant with curly black hair who loved children. He would come home every day at five o'clock, driving his car past our window and parking on the other side of the street.

My sister would be there waiting for Mel under the willow tree in front of his house. He would give her a big kiss and a hug, and she would talk to him, the most outrageous gibberish and lies, a blue streak. My sister as a child talked with the wit and steady volubility of a young Dorothy Parker. Mel called her "Curly Top."

"Curly Top" had a waterfall of personality which no one could resist. She became, eventually, much more outgoing and socially adventurous than I, who have always been satisfied with a few close friends.

On rainy days my sister and I sometimes played together. We played board games like Monopoly and checkers. One of our favorite games was making "forts" in nooks and crannies of the house, behind the couch, in closets, in the basement behind the unfinished wall paneling where my sister would set up housekeeping within, and I would arrange military fortifications without. The other game I remember with pleasure was appropriately literary. We would write notes to each other and pass these back and forth from the basement to the upstairs bedrooms through a hole beneath the radiator.

Rock-and-roll music always brought us together for "jam sessions," when we would play records and pound on any resonant furniture that was at hand. Our senses of humor were so similar we enjoyed many of the same comic television programs and the stories of James Thurber and Mark Twain. My mother would read to my sister and me before bedtime, all of us stretched out on the double bed in the master bedroom.

Younger siblings commonly imitate their older brothers and sisters. But this is much more common among siblings of the same sex. Cross-sex siblings are not nearly so imitative. My sister shared my love of language and my reading habits and, to some extent, my sense of humor. But as far as the rest of my personality was concerned, it seems to me, she played off against me as if I had been the model of everything harmful to her health and peace of mind. She managed to do this in spite of a decent measure of older-brother hero worship, which I received with the superior graciousness of a typical eleven-year-old, approving of her crayon drawings of me and basking in her praise of my guitar playing.

No sooner had she discovered who her brother was, than she began defining herself as all her brother was not.

The nuclear family is a glorious pressure cooker. Brothers and sisters call forth passions from one another without half trying. They nurture and threaten us. We see our siblings in such close quarters and get to know them so well, sharing the sustenance of life, that we grow to love and hate them as we will love and hate people only rarely outside the family circle.

Insofar as you agree with your sister, you may love her more than any friend you will ever know. When affection is good between siblings, it is very, very good. Sibling love that flourishes happily has become a proverbial ideal for friendship. So the proud friend boasts, "The two of us are like brothers," or "I loved her like a sister," or "We are like brother and sister." In each case, what the speaker means is that the two friends are like siblings who love each other, like David and Jonathan—not like hostile Cain and Abel, or Jacob and Esau.

Insofar as you differ from a brother, he may seem more alien to you than a Ubangi spearman. If your differences lead to hatred, this may be hatred more intense than any you could feel for a nonkinsman (with the possible exception of an ex-spouse). Knowledge is power, according to the old adage, and in no arena is this so heartbreakingly evident as in the family. Knowledge of our brothers and sisters fuels our love, as well as our hatred, for them.

We do not choose our brothers and sisters. Yet we must get to know them as well as any companions we have chosen out of love. There is, on the basis of temperament and personality, no more reason for us to love a sibling than any individual picked at random from our kindergarten class. Yet we have to go home with brother or sister. The shared experience and the home ought to unite us, yet these can seem to magnify our differences.

Perhaps this is why so little has been written about sibling love. People are generally proud of their love affairs, their marriages, the devotion to their children. But they often feel guilty about their ambivalence toward a sister or a brother, and so prefer not to publicize it.

The philosopher Aristotle, who wrote more wisely about friendship than anyone ever has before or since, offers a single sentence of doctrine about the love between siblings. He says, in brief, that brothers love each other as being born of the same parents: their identity with the parents makes them identical with each other. Hence, the phrase "the same blood." While this is a sweet and agreeable idea, it belongs more to the world of symbolic logic and mathematics than to the hothouse of the nuclear family.

So long as the family holds us captive, our feelings will grow, and ripen, beautifully or grotesquely. The family does not give us the freedom of choosing our company or abandoning one who annoys us. At its best, the affection between sister and sister, brother and brother, or brother and sister resembles the love between lifelong, elective friends. At worst, the bond between siblings imposes all the agonies of having an enemy for whom, by an accident of birth, you are ironically responsible. Those who can rise to the occasion may be rewarded in Heaven, but on earth there is no greater aggravation.

As we move from the consideration of sibling love to childhood friendship, we ought to understand how love differs, if at all, from friendship.

Fortunately we have Aristotle to help us.

He says, "It looks as if love were a feeling, and friendship a state of character."

No one could have put it plainer.

You may love a lifeless thing—a chair, a bracelet, or a map of Virginia; you may love the body of a woman or a man to whom you have never spoken. But a friend you love must love you back, the love must be mutual. Mutual love involves choice, and choice springs from a state of character. This is equally true of strangers and (may the good Lord help us) blood relatives.

C MY FIRST FRIEND

Childhood friends are like brothers and sisters in that they are often thrust upon us, before we have much choice in the matter.

My closest friend of early childhood was Paul Collodny. Paul came to stand, first on one foot, then the other, in our freshly sodded front yard, to watch the moving crew carry our furniture into the new house. The sturdy little boy lived across the street.

Paul looked as if he had been in a fight he had won at some cost: lumps on his forehead; swollen, narrow eyes; a Roman nose; and a big smile. He had not been in a fight; that was just the way he looked. Later he would explain the lumps on his brow as an excess of brains, a family trait, pointing to his older brother, Harry, who had the same lumps on his forehead. Paul would eventually become a ruggedly handsome young man, but as a kid he looked like old Rocky Marciano. A couple of years later I sort of accidentally hit Paul on the forehead with a baseball bat and raised a painful blue knot on his brow, which hardly anyone noticed among the congenital crags.

Paul and I played together every day from the eve of my fourth birthday until we were teenagers. We went to school together and came home together, though our parents wisely saw to it we were enrolled in different classes. The two of us shared everything we could share with each other for as long as we could. By the time we got to high school, our interests had grown so far apart that we held little in common other than our past, and nostalgia alone cannot carry a friendship into the open field of adulthood.

While that friendship lasted, ours was a model of its kind. Paul and his brother, Harry, two years older, were very close: they loved each other with that bittersweet affection I have come to associate with the best sibling bonds. Because I never had a brother, much of what I understand about brothers comes from growing up across the street from Paul and Harry. They shared, and quarreled, and were fiercely loyal to each other. Harry was "the handsome one." That is, he looked exactly like Paul, except his eyes opened a little wider and he had blond hair. Paul was the clever one, though they were both clever. They loved each other as much as any brothers do.

Now, more than thirty years later, I doubt that either man would dispute me if I say that Paul and I were, for ten years, just as close as the two blood brothers. Except for the night hours the brothers spent sleeping in their bunk beds, Paul and I spent more time together. Harry had his own friends, only two years older; but when you are children growing up, two years' difference in age can mean a lot. Paul and I knew the sweetness of companionship without bitterness. If things were not going well between us, we did not wait around for the situation to deteriorate. He went his way, and I went mine. We had a choice. Paul and Harry had no choice: they would always have to go home to the same dinner table and bedroom, the same mother and father.

What drew Paul and me together? Nothing much more specific than the landscape. We lived in a new housing development on what looked to us like the frontier: deep woods, rivers, fields, and orchards. Out the back door of Paul's house, in 1953, was an open field of several acres, bounded by a forest covering the miles of hills and valleys that followed the Sligo Creek. We were explorers turned loose upon the wilderness, with no instructions from our parents except their warning us not to get lost. We made maps and rafts, and buried treasures. Once in a while a child would get lost in the woods, and found again. This happened to me once, as snow fell and night came on. It seemed to me I was lost for an eternity before I heard my mother's voice faintly in the distance calling my name. After that I decided that I had better do all my exploring with a partner.

Paul and I were perfect partners in the wilderness. He was strong, enthusiastic, marvelously resourceful, and inventive. In our coonskin caps we would set out. If we built a fort in the woods, he was the architect. I would embellish the stockades with visions and stories of previous Indian inhabitants and Pilgrim ghosts, or specters of immediate enemies—cliff dwellers, mad hermits, escaped convicts hiding out in the woods. Paul was all business, he was the bricks and mortar department.

What held us together for ten years, as companions of choice? After all, the neighborhood was full of children our age.

Right next door to Paul and Harry lived Leonard Eisenberg, a slender, impishly handsome Jewish boy who was always perfectly groomed and dressed in new shirts and jeans without patches. Leonard was a fine playmate. The three of us played in a sandbox behind Leonard's house.

One day when we were about five years old, Leonard found, somewhere in the woods, a railroad spike. He amused himself by dropping it from above his head so the shiny spike would stick upright in the sandpile. Paul got his hand in the way of the falling railroad spike, which stuck upright in the sand anyway, slicing two little fingers almost free from his left hand in the wink of an eye.

Paul held his hand up, bleeding as the fingers dangled by a patch of skin, and Leonard ran away to hide in the woods. My mother rushed Paul to the hospital in time to get the fingers sewed back on so they would grow out right.

I missed Paul while he was laid up.

Leonard was heartbroken and needed as much consolation as Paul, who of course was getting not only the full treatment of sympathy which was his due, but the purple heart for courage and a hero's welcome home from the hospital. Leonard was a good boy who never would have hurt Paul on purpose. Paul forgave him, yet things were never quite the same between them after that. But they were both good boys who continued to play together.

We were all good boys most of the time. I do not remember a single case of deliberate cruelty on the part of any of those boys I grew up with—cruelty to animals or unkindness to other children. We simply would not have tolerated it: cruelty was no fun. Cracking each other's heads playing football without equipment, that was our idea of fun.

There were bad boys in the neighborhood, and we knew who they were and stayed away from them. They smoked cigarettes and tortured cats and killed robins with pellet guns. They cut school. They were mean to each other. Spitting and cursing, they roamed the same woods we did; and once in a while we heard that they "captured" a good boy, and took all of his clothes off, and tortured him. Their faces grew twisted. One day I could not avoid them; and while we waited for the school bus, one of the bad boys, laughing fiendishly, burned me in the back of the neck with the coal of his lighted cigarette.

But this was a rare incident, because the older good boys vigilantly protected the younger good boys from the bad boys. If you believe there is no such thing as a bad boy, you either have a short memory or you grew up in a world very different from mine. There were some really bad boys where I grew up. We learned to run away from them and to fight them when they caught us. These boys would become murderous, larcenous men, graduating from Loch Raven Reformatory to the Maryland State Penitentiary, where they now reside at my expense.

Out of the whole gang of good boys, Paul and I were best friends of choice, because of a peculiar harmony of temperaments, and similar values.

THE STAGES OF FRIENDSHIP

Paul Collodny and I, meeting at age five, took animal delight, moment by moment, in each other's physical actions, long before we had the faintest idea what caused the pleasure, or even that we could count upon it to continue from one day to the next.

Social awareness develops in stages, each stage representing a child's reorganization of mental elements.

At first, before the age of four, the child sees his playmate as a momentary physical companion. He reflects on the shape, movement, and sound of the playmate, but in these early years, imagination has not yet done the work of integrating time and the continuity of other people's characters. A good friend is just "someone who plays with me a lot," or "someone who lives on my street," or "someone who doesn't take things away from me."

At the second stage, reached by age five or six, the child understands his friend does things that please him. Paul let me play with his squirt gun. I pulled him in my wagon, and he liked that. He would share his ice cream. A friend must know what you like and dislike. Yet at this point we still had no understanding of the reciprocal nature of friendship.

Around the age of seven or eight, my friend Paul and I reached the third stage. At this point in their progress, the two candidates understand friendship is a two-way street, and each friend must adapt to the other's needs. This requires enough imagination to take the other person's point of view.

I loved athletics and was an obsessive year-round ball player. Paul was a capable but indifferent athlete, who would rather build a rocket ship out of orange crates in his backyard. I did not really care one way or the other about the rocket ship, but I would play apprentice to Paul's master builder all morning, knowing I could throw a baseball at him in the afternoon. Now looking back, I think that in his company I enjoyed the one game as much as the other.

I remember with particular affection our project of planting sweet-gum trees in his yard and mine. The two of us were in first grade and it was springtime, so we must have been six years old. I had seen the unusual trees in the woods, with their luxuriant broad leaves of deep green, and thought they would look good on our street. I suggested we uproot a couple of seedlings and transplant them, one in his yard and one in mine.

The tree planting was my idea, but I could not have carried it into action on my own. For all my athletic enthusiasm, I was clumsy at small tasks and not as well organized and handy as my friend. Paul got the shovel and bucket out of his basement and led us to the woods where he directed the excavation of the two saplings.

We passed the shovel back and forth, making sure we got all the roots and as much of the tree's own soil as the bucket would hold.

He chose a site in the center of his front yard, and did most of the digging there, though I spelled him from time to time. He covered the roots, danced on the fresh earth to pack it down, and sprinkled the tree with a watering can, while I nursed a blister on my thumb.

I chose the spot for my tree in our backyard, because there was already a big maple in front of my house. This time, because my hand was hurting me, Paul did all the shoveling. I watched him in admiration. Then we went inside my house and ate dinner together.

Paul's tree dried out and turned brown and died in the summer. My tree, which I prefer to call *our* tree, is still standing in that neighborhood where neither of us has lived for twenty years, and the trunk is so big around you could not span it with both arms. To me the tree represents the health of friendship that comes of similarities *and* differences, complementary temperaments, my vision and Paul's efficiency.

I like to think that Paul found me stimulating; I surely found him a great comfort. I had an enormous amount of nervous energy and anxiety and enough verbal imagination to keep both of us terrified in the woods and fields far from home.

Paul was steady and sturdy and mostly brave. He was wonderfully patient, in the way some children can be patient, with my anxieties and nerves and ineptitudes. I could not drive a nail. And my *conscience* kept meddling in our business, interfering with some of our bolder plans.

Yet Paul accepted my failings with humor. He was, in short, a kind of older brother to me.

Deep in the woods one day, Paul and I, intrepid explorers, came upon a hillock in a clearing. The raised earth was in the perfect shape of an enormous throne, and the light through the hemlock trees shone upon a circular floor of pine needles and twigs which looked like the throne room of some sylvan monarch.

Paul and I looked at each other in silent wonder.

I was the first to be frightened, but I suppose we were thinking more or less the same thing, given our family backgrounds.

"Monstrous Grayhair," I said gravely.

"What?"

"Monstrous Grayhair, the giant gorilla monster."

"Oh," said Paul, looking over his shoulder.

"This is his castle. And up there is where he sits when he gets home."

Wind moved in the trees overhead.

We were both hoping silently that the monster would not come home just yet. We wanted to explore his castle.

Behind the hill throne stood a pile of rusting beer cans. Paul's father was an alcoholic. Some days he was full of fun, singing so we could hear him across the street. But when he got sad he would keep Paul indoors, and they would not let me in. Paul's father would go away for days or weeks without warning. His unpredictable comings and goings were a constant worry for the whole family.

Though my father did not drink, he was just as scary as Paul's father.

Paul kicked at the pile of beer cans.

"I guess he's a drunk," said Paul.

I said I supposed he was.

"Hope he doesn't come back here drunk and find us," said Paul, his brave demeanor showing signs of fear. We found a pile of bleached bones from the monster's lunch. Just then a dog howled, and Paul and I got out of there fast, running through the forest paths and briars and thickets, running for our lives a few steps ahead of the seven-league strides of Monstrous Grayhair, feeling his horrible whiskey breath upon the backs of our necks, running until we reached my house, where we hid under the basement stairs, panting.

Paul and I, in the full ripeness of oedipal horrors, created an entire mythology of Monstrous Grayhair, the drunken gorilla monster. Taller than any skyscraper, he lived in the castle of the forest.

For months we thrilled at the mention of his name. We scouted Monstrous Grayhair through the hills and valleys, always just a few steps behind him. He drank cases of Miller beer at a sitting, squeezing the cans until the beer exploded into his greedy mouth—pop! pop! pop!—like a string of firecrackers. And then the beer would whet his appetite for small boys and large dogs. My family owned a cocker spaniel. Monstrous Grayhair had a particular fondness for spaniel meat. So it was our duty, when we were not reconstructing the movements and manners of Monstrous Grayhair in his neck of the woods, to prepare for the invasion of our homes.

We were the heroes of this romance, and our courage and ingenuity would eventually prevail. We set our minds to making a trap for the monster.

Paul was a brilliant inventor. After presenting various blueprints for land mines, mazes, bent-tree springs, and jungle pits, Paul convinced me of the superiority of his Standing Rake Trap. This was a miracle of deadly simplicity, elegant deceit. I had, in my basement, a long-handled steel rake, the kind used for thatching. We were so little that it took the two of us to lift the rake up the cellar stairs and stand it up on end where the weapon towered menacingly above us, twice our height. The trick was to balance the long rake on its handle, by a web of strings in the open gate, so the wicked teeth of the rake gaped above our heads against the blue sky. And, presumably, the rake would also loom above the head of Monstrous Grayhair, whose height our imaginations had conveniently diminished for this purpose. Anything twice as tall as a six-year-old boy must seem equally monstrous, whether it be a gorilla or a garden tool.

Now all we needed was bait. Booze was the answer. The gorilla was powerless to resist the hooch. But how would we arrange a beer can in such a way that the monster, groping for it, would pull the rake down upon his gray head and bury the steel teeth in his skull? I had an inspiration. Somewhere in my house I remembered there was a key charm in the shape of a tiny bottle of Seagram's gin. Paul said that gin would do just fine, so I went and got the little bottle for him.

As Paul balanced on the fence rail, I held his knees, and he slipped the key chain over one of the tines of the standing rake.

We could hardly go to sleep that night in our excitement, wondering if our trap would destroy, or put to flight, this hideous monster, in whose shadow the two of us had trembled for so long.

In the morning I looked out my bedroom window and could see the rake had fallen. I got dressed and ran out my door, across the street to Paul's house to get him out of bed.

The two of us hurried to the scene of the violent encounter between Monstrous Grayhair and his nemesis, the Standing Rake.

It was a total success, a victory that had put Monstrous Grayhair to rout, probably forever. The rake had fallen straight forward as we had designed it to do, and must have struck the giant gorilla such a painful blow that he did not even carry off the little bottle of Seagram's gin that had lured him to his doom. The bottle was still entangled in the tines of the rake, which were buried an inch in the soft ground.

As we told the story to each other, trading details, we began to feel almost sorry for the poor, defeated monster, nursing his bloody skull up there in his forest castle. He would never fool with us again.

So Paul Collodny and I were prepared, ahead of schedule, for the fourth and highest stage of childhood friendship.

This stage of childhood friendship displays a full-blown, intimate, and mutual sharing. By the time children are ten or eleven years of age, they fully understand that friendship grows over a period of months or years, in which two people prove their power to provide each other with affection and support. They know close friends need to "mesh" psychologically: They must have similar values and harmonious temperaments. Ultimately they learn to trust each other, knowing each is truly concerned with the other's welfare, and that their happiness is somehow entwined. Paul and I, very early, began to share our dreams and fantasies; he would become a great architect, and I would be President, the first Jewish President. We could tell each other anything in utter confidence.

This fourth phase of childhood friendship resembles adult friendship. As adults, we wish for our friends what is good for their sake. Yet there is an important difference between adult and childhood friendship. The feelings and dynamics may be similar—but, remember, friendship is not a feeling. Love is a feeling, a feeling that intimate friends have in some measure for each other; friendship, however, is a state of character, two characters to be exact, like a marriage. A child's personality grows as rapidly as his arms and legs, changing as unpredictably as his voice or hair coloring. So the likelihood of a child's closest friendship surviving adolescence is poor and slim. When this happens, as in our case, it is a blessed accident.

The sadness of childhood friendships is that we thoughtlessly leave them behind with other, less precious things of our evanescent youth. Paul and I did not see this coming. We were so proud and confident of our bond we did not need to name it. We were not jealous or exclusive. I spent a lot of time with Leonard Eisenberg, a better ball player than Paul. Leonard and I were friends, too. For all of Paul's patience with my obsessions, and his loyalty, he would not continue to play catch with the baseball until long after twilight, as Leonard would. Leonard and I would play until the baseball had become a white blur, and then just a sound, a faint buzzing just before the baseball hit the leather of your glove, or your head.

As Paul got older, his great kindness made him a natural den mother for the younger kids on the block. He spent time policing them, and teaching them things, and refereeing their games, while I was off playing basketball or baseball with Leonard or reading books.

I guess it was the books, finally, that came between us. But not until we were almost grown.

Books and Jews. I got to know these at about the same period of my childhood. My father was Jewish and wanted me to attend Hebrew school twice a week. The school behind the synagogue smelled like a library, except more intense because the books were thousands of years old.

In Hebrew school I discovered a group of boys who were

so formidably brainy I had to struggle to keep up with them. Two of them, Joe Klein and Merrill Bloom, were in my fourth-grade public school class. Joe was round and pigeon-toed and comical, a born mime. Bloom was angular and droll and hatchet-faced, with black kinky hair, a mathematical wizard. The three of us began competing for top scores in the daily exams, which Klein began handicapping as if the three of us were young racehorses.

Bloom and Klein, who lived on the same block, had grown up together as Paul and I had. And these two boys were rather clannish, Jewish chauvinists. They forgave me for having a Christian mother, but they might not have forgiven me so easily had I not been able to do two-place multiplications in my head and hit a baseball well out of the infield.

They were polite to my friend Paul. But he was sensitive enough to know that off the baseball field they were just tolerating him, that Paul was not of their element. He never complained, though once in a while he would tease me about the weirdness of my Hebrew chanting around the Chanukah candles. He would beg me to put my "beanie" on my head, my black yarmulke. And when I would finally give in and put on the prayer cap, he would fall on the floor and roll about laughing, laughing much harder than he would have laughed if he had not felt somehow excluded.

Paul's parents were Baptists. I used to tag along with Paul and Harry when they went to youth prayer meetings at the church, where the boys and girls would talk about blood and crucifixion and the Saviour's suffering, and how they would all be royal ambassadors of Christ. They had purple armbands and got me one too, though they knew I would not wear it.

A couple of years later, when we entered junior high school, the crowd we ran with was almost entirely Jewish. And Paul was wholly accepted, an honored guest at bar mitzvahs—but he was well aware that he was different, and that his strangeness had something to do with books and language and values.

About the same time I fell in with the Jews, or perhaps a year or two earlier, I discovered books. Ironic, now that I think about it: the book that first took over my life was *Huckleberry Finn,* Harry's copy of the book, which he had just finished and recommended. I got the book off the shelf under the east window of the brothers' bedroom, stretched out on the lower bunk bed, and started reading. I could not be moved. It was summertime, and the boys left me there with the book while they went out into the backyard to play baseball.

To make a long story short, I got interested in books, and the ideas in them, and then in the things one could discover or understand only through reading books. I began to read for two or three hours a day, which is a big chunk out of a boy's life. When I got done reading, I wanted action, intense physical action—some pick-up basketball or a bone-rattling game of football; and as I said earlier, Paul was less interested in sports. He was still building things—woodcrafts in his basement, radios, and go-carts with old lawn-mower engines. Later it would be automobile engines, which were as boring to me as my philosophy books were to Paul.

At twelve years of age, Paul got lost in a Briggs and Stratton two-cycle gasoline motor, and I began studying Hume's *Inquiry Concerning Human Understanding.* The more complex our different obsessions became, the more trouble we had relating to each other day to day. And before we knew it, we had stopped trying.

Most of us during the course of a lifetime experience three kinds of friendship.

All of us know the friendship of "utility," where two people band together because of some good they get from each other, like business partners or their clients. Then there is the friendship of pleasure, in which two people love each other for the sake of delight: you may take pleasure in a friend simply because she makes you laugh or is nice to look at. These first two kinds of friendship are only incidental and, ultimately, disappointing. People who love for the sake of utility, love only for the sake of what is good for *themselves*; likewise, the folks who love for pleasure, these love only what is agreeable to themselves. Such friends will love you only so long as you are useful to them, or entertaining. Such friendships fail the test of time, because the useful is always changing, and so are the things that make us pleasant—health, beauty, rollicking humor.

The only kind of friendship that truly deserves the name, is a third kind, which the philosophers call *perfect friendship*. This is the friendship of two people who are good and, as Aristotle says, like each other in virtue. For friends like these wish each other well for no reason apart from their individual goodness. "Those who wish well to their friends for *their* sake are most truly friends; for they do this by reason of their own nature and not incidentally; therefore their friendship lasts as long as they are good—and goodness is an enduring thing."

The friendship of children, and most young people, aims at pleasure. Paul Collodny and I were drawn together by an animal delight in each other's presence. But we *continued* to be friends of choice because of certain similarities of virtue. Paul was goodhearted in a way that made him outstanding in a group of honorable boys. He had high regard for the truth in intimate matters, and he showed a passion for truth in exploring the natural and mechanical world. He had courage that surpassed mine.

If Paul lacked anything in the way of character as an adult, it was self-knowledge. He was much brighter and more capable than he ever knew. Loyal friends were powerless to assure him of his talents, though we elected him president of the senior class. He was a good student who should have been superior. I think Paul was suspicious of college and all ideas upon which I would base my life, the supreme importance of inquiry and the pursuit of beauty, while I became uncomfortable with his social, and more practical, ambitions.

If I had been a better friend or as goodhearted as he was, I might have made a greater effort to close the gap between us. But the two of us were so busy, each in his own world, we never realized what we might be losing. We still saw each other several times a week—coming and going in the halls of high school or on our street, where we would catch up on each other's lives while visiting girls together or shooting baskets at the neighborhood court.

Then high school graduation came, and geography separated us forever. No matter how much we may have loved each other, the two states of our characters would never regain their common border.

I have heard that Paul and his brother Harry live near each other and get along as well as they ever did. I'm not surprised, for they were always more like each other than I was like either of them. Between Paul and me, on the other hand, the potential for rivalry might have led to disaster. In our high school class of nine hundred, I was president of the class the first year, and Paul the last. We became distinctly different physical and emotional types; and though I think we would still harmonize temperamentally, he would have no patience with my intellectual habits, nor I with his mechanics and business preoccupations.

But how would we manage if we were brothers, and the family kept calling us together? My guess is that we would come to the table, and love each other as in childhood, but with the added bitterness of two people so familiar they cannot deny their differences, their failures, or help but regret they have grown apart. We would come together, and do all for each other that love and responsibility command. But this would not be easy. Love never is easy for brothers, even those as lucky as Paul and Harry.

BOYS AND GIRLS

Bicycles were our tickets to freedom; and when Paul and I were old enough to own full-size bicycles, we began to enlarge our circle of acquaintances. Together, we discovered girls.

We were as fortunate in this as we had been in meeting each other at age four. The girls we met when Paul and I were eleven, lived within easy walking distance, and they grew up to be such fine women that they made good friends to us, and to one another, until high school graduation sent us our separate ways.

We discovered these girls in the summer of our seventh-grade year, just before we graduated from elementary school to junior high school. During our six years of elementary school, Paul and I had little to do with girls. While doing the informal research for this book, I asked my mother whether there had been any girls in the neighborhood as we were growing up, because I could not remember any. She told me that there were, but that Paul and Harry and Leonard and I paid no attention to the girls whatsoever. They might as well have been in another dimension, the girls, playing jump rope and hopscotch, in the street or indoors. They did not go into the woods, where we spent most of our time.

We certainly had our dreams and fantasies about them, and crushes on certain pretty girls in school. Paul had a sister two years younger, and I remember "double-swinging" with her on the playground. She was pretty, and I found swinging double with her agreeable and unsettling, unmistakably erotic.

In elementary school gym class we had, every year, a month of square dancing which the girls loved and the boys all pretended to hate, and certain girls were more pleasant to swing around and promenade than others. But girls in general, taking one with another, were just too strange a species for us to have any regular interest in them. They giggled to no purpose and held hands. They wanted to kiss you or each other. On the playground they sang, and they threw funny. Not a single one of them could throw a baseball without putting the wrong foot forward.

Now I know all of this has changed since Paul and I were pre-adolescents. But when we were children in the 1950s, boys acted like boys, and girls acted like girls, and the exceptions were truly exceptional.

In the summer of 1960, coasting home in the twilight from a marathon bike ride, we discovered Annie Berman. She was sitting on the steps of a house on the far end of our very own block. Amazing that we had never noticed her before sitting there. She had probably waved to us, and smiled, a dozen times. Annie was a slender, energetic girl with a headful of black curls, a high forehead, a long nose and chin, and dark, sparkling eyes. Her smile was always accomplished with some effort because Annie's mouth, a beautifully shaped little rosebud, was rather small.

This time Paul waved, and I smiled, and we curbed our bicycles in front of Annie Berman's house.

We found out that Annie Berman, who had been going to a different elementary school, would be going to junior high school with us, on the same bus. The three of us talked until dark, though Paul and Annie did most of the talking, while Annie and I mostly just looked at each other and looked away again. Annie was the very definition of vivacity and friendliness, and she laughed easily. She made us feel we were the most important people in the neighborhood.

We left her at nightfall, agreeing to get together the next day.

We got together the next day, and the next, and Annie introduced us to some of her girlfriends, Cindy Myers and the twin sisters Betty and Rachel Honig, who looked as much like each other as Stan Laurel and Oliver Hardy. Cindy was round and dark-skinned and very funny, like Annie; the two of them were as close as Paul and I were.

These girls all came from model Jewish families of the lower-middle-class suburbs of the 1950s. They were not "princesses" by any stretch of the imagination. Their parents welcomed Paul and me and our boyfriends into their homes with as much generosity as any parents of adolescent girls have ever welcomed adolescent boys. Soon the whole gang of us were living in and out of each other's houses. We soon discovered these girls had many of the same virtues we appreciated in each other, with the added power to make us feel particularly good about ourselves—smarter, braver, and more handsome. They seemed to envision greatness in us, and we did not ever want to disappoint them.

For the next six years no mother ever had to wonder where her child had gone. We were with one another.

Of all these girls, Annie was my best friend. She is, indeed, the one friend of childhood with whom I maintain contact, long-distance. So here I should say a little more about Annie Berman, and what I felt for the dark-haired girl who lived down the street, and in whose home I spent so many happy hours of my adolescence.

Annie Berman and I were as harmonious, from the beginning, as were Paul Collodny and I. In fact, the strengths of Annie's character sound like a list of Paul's—the kindness, the sympathetic understanding, the courage in the face of all the trials of young adulthood. She had a better sense of humor than Paul. The two of us would easily fall into Marx brothers–style repartee. She had more imagination and self-understanding than Paul.

I could tell her anything, from the problems my parents were having with each other to my embarrassment about pimples. And Annie would always listen, with her head cocked to one side, reflecting to find exactly the words that would make me feel better.

Paul and I both loved Annie from the day we met her. But there was no jealousy. Paul—being the person you know him to be, and a little older than Annie—immediately assumed the role of her "older brother." He had a big brother, as well as a younger sister, so Paul was familiar with the role. Annie had no older brother and always wanted one. Before long, Paul and Annie had agreed upon the sibling connection, and proudly verbalized it, and that was how they loved each other from then on.

As for me, my feelings for Annie would become far more complicated. I spent more time with her, going to synagogue, getting invited to Passover seders and Rosh Hashanah feasts. We listened to records and read poetry. She was just as good a friend as Paul, but I was soon in love with her.

B ANOTHER MYSTERY

Before I leave the discussion of sibling love and childhood friendship, I want to say a little more about the mystery of these kinds of bond. If the purpose of life is learning, and love is the Great Educator, what are we supposed to learn from loving our siblings and the friends of childhood? Some of us have no siblings. Can we suppose that an only child knows less about love than the rest of us?

For those who believe that the varieties of love are different forms of a single entity, this question becomes less troublesome. If fate has denied you the experience of one form of love, another form may compensate for the loss.

Those of us with siblings have an advantage in learning. Brotherhood compels us to endure the company of another soul we must admit as equal to us in value. Our knowledge of sisters and brothers is so intimate we must acknowledge their hopes, their fears, their sufferings as being as vivid and real as our own. They are the first "others" we encounter who are equal to us, and we must love them in spite of the bitterness they often inspire.

What is love teaching us in the nuclear family? Love is teaching us, by main force, to see siblings as equals in value, and to respect them no matter how much or little we love them. Sibling love teaches us to love humankind, taking the bitter with the sweet, preparing us for altruism in the greater world.

Childhood friendship accomplishes the same end. For even a chosen friend has shortcomings we tolerate; and even an only child learns tolerance in handling a playmate who is thrust upon him. Perhaps the chief legacy of childhood friendship between nonsiblings or kin, is this: The process, from physical attraction to mutual caring, becomes the model for adult friendship and conjugal love.

Let us approach, with some caution, one more mystery.

Paul Collodny and I met on the eve of my fourth birthday, and grew up directly across the street from each other. We had perfectly harmonious temperaments. We went to a large suburban public high school and graduated in a class of nine hundred students, of which I was class president the sophomore year, and Paul was elected senior class president two years later. We did not campaign for or against each other. We were too busy.

What, in the name of all that is probable and holy, were the odds that two class presidents, in a school of three thousand students from a radius of fifteen miles, would have grown up across the street from each other? Of course, we did not plan it. And at the time this hardly seemed worthy of comment to us, though the neighborhood made the coincidence a popular topic of conversation, as if we had been Thomas Jefferson and John Adams, and the local council might rename our street the Avenue of the Presidents.

Everybody knows, or else should know, that those two famous Americans Adams and Jefferson, intimate lifelong friends, died within hours of each other on July 4, 1826, exactly a half-century after the signing of the Declaration of Independence.

Friendship seems to occasion striking coincidences. Lately in a small town in the Midwest, journalists discovered a high school basketball team they were hailing as a state championship contender, in a big populous state with three or four hundred large suburban high schools. There were articles about the phenomenon in the major media. This small town with one church, a dozen houses, and a gasoline pump somehow produced an All-American basketball team out of a tiny high school, with only a few more boys than fit on the varsity squad. These guys had grown up with one another, shooting baskets and playing pickup games in a vacant lot. Basketball drew them together, like to like, and friendship bonded them.

Paul and I, friends almost from infancy, would not have become the people we have become without learning certain lessons from each other and from our friendship. Perhaps another child might have served me just as well as Paul, but I doubt it. The two of us were just plain lucky—at least, I know I was.

The poet Homer says, "God is ever drawing like towards

like, and making them acquainted." Fate casts certain people in our paths—sisters, brothers, neighbors. Perhaps the best friends arrive when we most need them.

EDUCATION

One of my favorite definitions of the truth comes from an old black philosopher. He sat in an alley in West Baltimore in the late nineteenth century, leaning back in a kitchen chair against the brick wall of a carriage house. This old gentleman sat there with a book in his lap, and he would interrupt his reading and cogitating from time to time to answer the questions of young folks.

One of the young folks was a little white boy who would grow up to be a notorious disturber of the peace, with his sense of mischief and raw common sense, calling himself a "critic of ideas." The white boy, who was named Henry Louis Mencken, once asked the grizzled philosopher what was truth.

The old man looked up from his book.

"The truth is what nobody but a damned fool will deny," said the black philosopher, and went back to his reading.

The boy scratched his head. With all his faith in the sage's wisdom, Henry Louis Mencken had expected a longer speech.

"How," the boy continued, "do you know the fools—"

"Because they deny it," said the old man, and resumed studying.

For all the circularity of the argument, the basic structure of it satisfies me.

In our lifelong process of seeking the truth, love is the kindly Professor as well as the Author of the Curriculum. That vibration whose pure form I first perceived in my grandmother's house is bound and determined to teach us the most important things we can know in this world. Because love enlightens us, philosophers and theologians have often imagined love as a teacher, with arms and legs and human language, with and without a blackboard behind her, or perhaps propping up the wall of a stable in an alley of West Baltimore.

This seems to be the truth. And though as children we understood nothing of philosophy, somehow we understood that love had something to teach us, Harry and Paul, my sister and me, in bringing us together to nourish each other and drawing us apart so we might change and grow.

Whatever else might have confounded us, there was always truth to be found in love, and we would be damn fools to deny it.

three

EROTIC LOVE

LUST AND EROS

This is the spring of my fortieth year. The April sunlight has brought the daffodils and hyacinths out of the earth right on schedule, and the air feels warm enough for folks to leave their coats at home.

This year some of the young women are wearing short skirts. I like that. I like especially the way the wind swirls the skirt up around her bright thighs, as that young woman in a low-cut peasant blouse turns the corner. She is clearly in a hurry, maybe on her way to meet somebody. Her limbs shine with an amazing radiance.

I am going to be forty years old in October, and I have a beautiful wife and two children. I am as happy with my family as a man can be. I do not have any idea who that woman is who just turned the corner, the one with the long legs and eyelashes. But I would like to engage her attention for just long enough to persuade her that on such a gorgeous day it would be sheer ingratitude on our part, gross contempt for the glories of nature and human possibility, if the two of us did not seek out a shelter of bushes in the nearby park.

And there we could shed these ridiculous clothes, and get as close to each other as our mortal bodies allow.

I will not do that. Twenty years ago, though, I would have done that, and in the late 1960s the odds of success would have been pretty good. Good enough that if I had engaged the attention of four or five healthy women, one of them might have taken the initiative upon herself. After all, this is spring, the midday moon is full, and of all occupations, none is more pleasant than making love. Or being with someone who makes you want to make love.

For almost eighteen years I have been with one woman who makes me want to make love. This is one of the reasons I turned away from that honey-haired stranger who vanished in a swirl around the corner. My wife is infinitely desirable. I suppose I am lucky in that, for how was I to know? I rather suspected she was infinitely desirable, which is one of the reasons I married her; but I am getting ahead of myself in the discussion of erotic love. Strictly speaking, my wife belongs in the chapter on conjugal love, which includes and transcends Eros.

Erotic love begins in an impulse for possession, an urge to follow a beautiful creature around a corner. But where does it end? Erotic love ends in possession, the moment in which a lover becomes one with the object he or she desires. At forty years of age, I am not compelled to follow that woman around the corner, because I have turned that particular corner more often than I care to admit. The thing of hers I most want to possess is a sweet thing I have possessed so many times I have learned I can do without the momentary satisfaction it affords. I do not know how anyone else comes to this, but that is how I learned it.

Of all the ways of love, erotic love is the most intense, dramatic, and impossible to ignore. The feeling makes your body throb. As such, Eros exists in relation to the other forms of love, as rock-and-roll music to all other forms of music. You may or may not like rock-and-roll music, but you cannot ignore the sound or mistake it for Brahms. You may be immune or insensitive to the chromatic subtleties of Maurice Ravel or the architecture of a Bach fugue; but you would have to be stone deaf or catatonic to resist the back beat and bass rhythm of the Rolling Stones or Chuck Berry. I have seen very old men and women protest that they hated rock-and-roll, and then tap their feet unconsciously to Chuck Berry. He makes music to raise the dead.

Likewise erotic love is love to raise the dead. Of course, most of us are very much alive. But Love, the professor, will not be taking any chances with the psychic health of his students, as he wishes all of us might pass his course. If any of us appear to be daydreaming or dozing, and he cannot get our attention with a cap pistol, he will use a twelve-gauge shotgun.

At age seven, Paul Collodny and I may have understood, intuitively, that love had a message for us; Annie Berman and I, ripening into adulthood, spent many an hour discussing the lessons of Eros.

CASANOVA, DON JUAN, AND COMPANY

I was born in the late 1940s. And so I arrived at sexual maturity just in time for the sexual revolution of the late 1960s.

Not everything people tell you about the 1960s is true, but it is true that young people in those years enjoyed unprecedented sexual freedom. Journalists did not call us the "love generation" for nothing. Orgasms resounded from the Atlantic to the Pacific like the gunfire of an earlier and less pleasant American revolution. The availability of efficient birth control methods, and the relative freedom from fear of diseases and divine retribution, created an atmosphere of magnificent erotic density.

I have often thought that if I had been born a decade later or earlier, my shyness and overdeveloped moral sense would have relegated me to a narrow experience of sexual pleasures. As it happened, the climate of the 1960s encouraged me to make love with every woman I found attractive. I find women to be generally attractive, and twenty years ago I was less discriminating than I am now. I thought women were, by and large, beautiful; time permitting, I made love with every beautiful woman I could persuade to return my affection. In the 1960s and early 1970s there seemed to be few who needed much persuading.

But this is not the time to launch into an account of my sexual antics and escapades à la Casanova. It really is not all that interesting, and this is not that kind of book. I was never like Casanova or Don Juan or Frank Harris, for I never shared their obsession with conquest. I was busy with things that do not much concern the great titans of fornication—things like falling in love. During the height of the sexual revolution, I fell in love with remarkable women who held my interest for years at a time. When someone is deeply in love with one man or woman, the lover has neither time nor attention to focus upon a lot of other objects of desire.

As long as his name has come up, let me say a few words about Casanova. Giovanni Jacopo Casanova (1725–98), the Italian adventurer, was expelled from his seminary in Venice at age sixteen for some scandalous conduct. He then embarked upon a checkered career as journalist, soldier, spy, alchemist, diplomat, and businessman, occupations that crossed and crisscrossed the map of Europe before retiring him to Bohemia, where he served as a librarian. There the libertine wrote his memoirs in twelve volumes, and died at the age of seventy-three, widely unmourned.

Casanova had many occupations and a single true vocation: He was a seducer of women. Women, according to Casanova, were his cuisine. He employed every imaginable trick to lure women to his "banquet bed," writing poetry for them, playing upon his violin, and exaggerating his prowess in all arenas of male endeavor.

Usually Casanova made love to the wives and daughters of his friends and patrons. Whenever possible, he tackled two women at once, so as to save time in transportation. His famous *Memoirs,* which provide a brilliant panorama of eighteenth-century life among the aristocracy, would convince us that before the age of forty-nine, when his narrative draws to an end, the hero had enjoyed the favors of several thousands of women.

Of course, no reader in his right mind would mistake such monkey business for love that is worthy of the name. The Freudians, always quick with explanations of human idiosyncrasy, have made short work of Casanova and his kind, by claiming the man was truly in love with his mother; and since he could not make love to his mother, Casanova must seduce woman after woman and then deny them, as he denied his lust for his mother. I do not accept this theory. I knew one man who behaved like Casanova but had no mother at all, and I knew another who hated his mother.

What we are witnessing in the Casanovas of this world, and their female counterparts (which are rare), are problems of erotic development.

Some consideration of lust and Eros, particularly Eros as it pertains to "generation," will offer us a clear explanation of

Casanova's obsession. His calling women a kind of food makes his problem even more obvious and all the more transparent. A roast beef is a dead thing which has no future. Casanova can desire this, and then possess it by ingestion, without any concern for the future of the roast beef or himself. A woman is not a roast beef; she has a future. If Casanova had any awareness that the woman was different from the roast beef, he could not so easily have gotten out of bed and left her, as though she had been consumed, like a gourmet dinner.

One may behave like Casanova at nineteen and be excused for not yet having learned the lessons of love. But the bedroom is a good study, and by the age of forty Casanova has no excuse. The pursuit of bodily beauty ought to have led him climax by climax to an awareness of generation—at least physical, if not spiritual.

An orgasm may be perceived in two ways: as a final, obliterating death or as a moment of regeneration. Eros works, through generation, toward the discovery of continuity of past and future. For most of us, the orgasm happily connects the past and the future. Poor Casanova—for him the pursuit of physical beauty remains utterly vain, because his moment of possession, of climax, is disconnected from the future. Connected to nothing, the moment implodes, creating a solipsistic black hole. In that intense moment the lonely Casanova dies an eternal death. And the woman might as well have been dead from the first, for she never had any future life of which Casanova was aware.

Of course, the legendary figure of the obsessive woman chaser is Don Juan, the central figure of dozens of plays before Mozart captured him in the great opera *Don Giovanni* in 1787.

The modern philosopher Ortega y Gasset, commenting upon the phenomenon of *Don Juanism*, tells us that real love is "centrifugal": that is, the feeling goes out from the lover to the beloved, from *me* to the *other*. Desire, as distinct from true love, has a sort of passive character. When I desire something, I really want the object to come to *me*.

And there you have the perfect picture of Casanova, the center of gravity, luring women to fall into his banquet bed. Strictly speaking, he is no lover at all. *Don Juanism* is desire without love; love would inspire him to move *toward* a woman temporally, if not spiritually. Instead, he flies continually from the souls and destinies of women who want to love *him*. Casanova has not learned the first lessons of Eros. Erotic love begins in physical desire, sexual lust to possess the beauty of another body—but the nature of erotic love is to lead us beyond the moment of physical possession, toward an everlasting generation.

I have enjoyed sex with a beautiful woman for the sheer pleasure of it, a woman I knew hardly at all and will probably never meet again.

She had long dark hair and eyes of china blue. I knew she was beautiful, and that was all I needed to know about her at the time. We met on a bus and two hours later were in her hotel room to spend the night. Yet I remember a certain sadness, as we rose together in the dim light of morning, as I watched her dressing. Her body was perfectly rounded, and full. She seemed then even more beautiful than she had been the night before. And I was curious about how she would spend this day without me, and how she would live the rest of her life. I wondered what her children would look like. I believe we shared a sense of longing, of unfinished business.

I was very young then, and I would have to repeat the experience with different women until the bitterness of it came to caution me against the pleasure. This is not morality. It is a clear preference based upon an understanding that erotic love is not meant to be satisfied by casual sexual union. The Turkish pasha, who has an innumerable handpicked harem at his disposal to gratify his every wish, eventually gravitates toward one woman. Sex is the early act of a much longer and more satisfying drama, as the desires of two people cross over and become lasting love. Though I dabbled in the pleasures of a Casanova in my early youth, I cannot imagine .taking much satisfaction in them today. I have also lost my taste for candied apples and jelly beans.

FALLING IN LOVE

Falling in love is very serious business whenever it happens. Eros is trying to get your attention, with the power of a shotgun, trying to get *through* to you for your own good, and you'd better listen. Falling in love is not to be ignored, laughed off, wished away, or dismissed as foolishness, which it sharply resembles.

You are born lucky if you fall in love only when you are "supposed to": that is, when you are young, free, healthy; when your beloved feels the same way about you; and when society showers you with blessings. Alas, almost nobody is born that lucky. Most of us, at one time or another, fall in love at the wrong time with the wrong person. Eros does not inspire us at our convenience. The spirit has much more pressing concerns.

"Falling in love" is an excellent phrase conveying the passive nature of the experience. You feel out of control, as if you were falling through space. We get even more mileage out of the words if we recall Ortega's belief that love is "centrifugal"—the feeling goes out from you to the one you love. You are falling out of yourself and toward them: the *beloved* becomes the center of gravity, not you.

In America we have another vivid term—"crush." You get a "crush" on someone you admire, with whom you would like to fall in love. The crush begins as a one-way proposition, usually secret, and narcissistic. It needs no help. When you have a crush on someone, you may think about him or her to the exclusion of everything else—food, work, play. You want to be alone to contemplate the hair and eyes of your beloved, while listening to sad music. You grow pale and hollow-eyed. You may lose a lot of weight, because you have lost your appetite in dreaming day and night about your beloved; and because the less flesh you have, the closer you come to pure spirit, which flies then to your beloved more easily. You long to be with the blessed one. But this is a delicious erotic longing, sweet pain you might actually prefer to the person's presence. When the glorious creature actually enters the room, your voice hides in your throat, you trip over a shoelace in trying to open the far door for her to exit—it is the door to the broom closet.

We think of this sort of crush as foolish behavior normal only to teenagers and stock characters in TV comedy. But it has vital significance. A lover becomes an "expert" in the perfections of his beloved. He sees the man or woman as God might regard His angels, untainted by mortal flaws. This is essential investigation and reflection, valuable for both lover and beloved, as the lover's vision works to remove the beloved from the impurity of Adam, to raise the beloved from the Fall.

Children giggle about crushes, though they understand love's seriousness, for they begin to suffer from it early. Cynics, who are children grown sour, dismiss falling in love as a snare and a delusion. Wise adults know better, and cope with the phenomenon in many ways, the most realistic being a prompt and clear confession to the beloved—*if* circumstances will allow this. When the passion is not reciprocated, the two grown-ups have a good hearty laugh, one with tears in his eyes, and the "crush" in time fades away.

A crush usually has a short life, because the lover contains it, smothering the passion. Eros, being a "centrifugal" force, requires room to grow, wants to get on with things outside, wants to generate in the beloved. One of the reasons a crush can be so intense is that the lover pressurizes and crushes inside him an emotion designed to populate the world.

When I was in graduate school, I had the worst kind of crush on a fellow student. She was beautiful, classically beautiful, tall and elegant, with thick blond hair and strong Scandinavian features, squarely defined. She was fabulously well educated, more evolved intellectually than any person my age I had ever encountered. That combination of beauty and brains was more than I could resist; she remains a marvel. I fell in love with her at first sight. No sooner had I been introduced to the woman than she began to haunt me.

Or perhaps it would be more accurate to say I haunted her. Her image got so firmly lodged in my mind I could hardly see anything else. I was convinced that this was the woman of my dreams, that she was made for me and I for her. So I discovered where she studied, and where she went for coffee and lunch, and where she lived. I thought about her in all of those places, and if I could I would show up nearby to strike up a conversation. She seemed to enjoy this. As we were studying many of the same subjects—poetry, philosophy— there was never any shortage of things to talk about. And I was never so witty, so animated, so *charming,* I thought, as when I was in this woman's presence.

However much she appreciated my jumping up in her path, day after day, like a jack-in-the-box, she could not have appreciated this as much as I believed she must. I had such a crush on her I never dreamed she would not soon feel the same way about me.

It even seemed incidental to me that she was already married. I thought about her all the time. Her husband could not possibly have thought about her as much as I did, or have loved her half as much. In the world of my love for her, he was a housefly. I remembered every word she ever spoke to me, and I rehearsed our conversations in my head and analyzed them word by word. I knew her perfections, surely, as only her mother might know them.

I lost fifteen pounds so as to make a better spirit to haunt her. At some point, I was certain, she would see that the two of us were dying for love of each other; she would rush into my arms like Anna Karenina, and the two of us would do what had to be done.

Of course, I never told her aloud what I was feeling. Somewhere in the vortex of this madness, I retained a finger-hold on propriety. My manners were perfect, courtly even.

After four or five months of this mooning and pining away, when the crush had driven me to the edge of distraction, I wrote the beautiful woman a short letter. I walked around the letterbox three or four times before dropping the letter in, and then nearly lost my arm in the slot as I tried to retrieve what I had written.

She wrote me back at once, an even shorter letter than mine. Her kind but absolutely firm letter left no question in my mind that what I had been feeling all those months had no equivalent in her own heart. She told me that it would be better if we did not see each other any more.

That was all I needed. Almost immediately I snapped out of it. I ate a huge dinner of steak and potatoes and ice cream, and resumed working as I had not worked in half a year.

Now, so many years later, I am certain this experience was a genuine inspiration of Eros, sustained, powerful, and nearly out of my control. What was the purpose? What was the spirit trying to teach me, that required so long and cruel a course of study? At the time I had no idea, except that the incident stood as a harsh reproof to my monstrous egotism.

All I could think about was what a drooling baboon I had made of myself.

Time has helped me to understand what happened, and the lesson may apply to unrequited crushes in general. The beautiful graduate student was not only beautiful; she was truly wise and good. She was not playing with me; she really wanted to be my friend. I remained content, for several months, to love this woman purely, spiritually, without laying a hand on her, and with no persuasive evidence she would ever return my love. During this period I was virtually celibate, as devoted to my ideal as Sir Galahad. This had never before happened to me as an adult. Previously the women I most desired usually desired me—in fact, this was a force that drew me to them; and as we possessed each other sexually, my soul was never put to such an agonizing test as I experienced when I was a graduate student. Then Eros required me to love this unattainable woman without recompense or carnal satisfaction. Insofar as I managed to do this for four months, my affections would benefit for the rest of my life.

EROS AND CUPID

Falling in love with someone who is falling in love with you is far more pleasant and infinitely more interesting.

When this happens immediately upon meeting someone, or just after, we call it love at first sight. "Our eyes met, our hands met, our lips met . . . and we knew then and there that nothing in Heaven or upon earth would ever come between us . . ." Well, well, well. The hushed crowd makes way for the lovers, acknowledging the miracle.

This is erotic love at its most potent: full strength, one-hundred-proof Eros. If you have never experienced it, the feeling is like the sudden weightlessness you sometimes experience in a high-speed elevator. You are literally in free-fall, the two of you—your bodies are falling away momentarily to give your spirits a chance to embrace before the bodies get into the act as well. This is why the eyes first experience the rush—the eyes being windows of the soul. The souls are engaged, hands take hold in order to maintain some balance in the fall, and then lips meet as the first point of contact for physical nourishment. It is a feast for the gods. You leave the party . . .

This does not happen very often. But when it does, the effect is so dramatic as to cast all other forms of love into the shade. Love at first sight has brought us *Romeo and Juliet, Tristan and Iseult,* and the romance of Robert and Elizabeth Barrett Browning. The phenomenon has also called forth a library of fascinating doctrine, as various lovers have struggled to make sense of the upheaval in their own lives.

The ancient Romans would say that those two lovers who just met at the party did not fall in love all by themselves. Hovering above them, near a chandelier, was a plump, smiling cherub held aloft by lacy wings, while he drew his ivory bow and transfixed each of the lovers' hearts with invisible arrows.

The Roman god Cupid is thoughtless, capricious, and silly. He will shoot his mischievous arrows at anyone he likes, ready or not, and make the victim fall in love with a suitor, a prostitute, or a pack mule, whatever amuses him. Seldom does Cupid shoot two people at once who fall in love with each other. That is too boring for Cupid, unless one of the candidates is already married, or one is sixty years older than the other, or the two are fighting against each other for the world heavyweight boxing title.

Cupid is *not* to be confused with Eros, who looks more like the young Socrates and really does have our best interests at heart.

Conveniently, the greatest single contribution to the doctrine of love is also the first: Plato's *Symposium*. Fortunate, that this is the first celebrated discussion of Eros, because the *Symposium* also undertakes to explain Eros's relation to other forms of love. We think of erotic love as being physical, but it is far more than that.

Plato describes love as a spirit (daemon) joining gods and humankind. Love is not mortal, nor immortal. Love is a great spirit intermediate between the divine and the mortal. Love interprets between gods and men. O gracious spirit! It carries our prayers to the gods, and the gods' commands and answers back down to us mortals.

If these words ring a bell for you, maybe it is because Plato's description of the spirit Eros became a blueprint for Jesus Christ of the New Testament.

As described by Plato in the *Symposium*, Eros is the son of the god Plenty and the goddess Poverty. Plenty, who once had a drop too much to drink at a party, fell asleep in Zeus's garden. Poverty, who came to the door to beg, found Plenty stretched out among the tulips and gardenias. Considering her own straitened circumstances, Poverty plotted to have a child by the god Plenty. So she lay down by his side and conceived Eros.

Like any child, Eros resembles his parents. He is not particularly beautiful, not the cherub on Valentine's Day cards. But then he is not ugly either. Eros is rough and squalid and has no shoes. He sleeps under the open sky, in the streets, or on doorsteps. Like his mother, Poverty, he is always in need.

Like his father, Plenty, he plots and schemes to ruin the fair and good. Those who are born with the advantages of beauty and virtue must be tested more strenuously than the rest of us; and if riches do not bring on their downfall, love may do the job.

Eros is bold, enterprising, strong, a mighty hunter (with that quiver of deadly arrows); he is always working at some intrigue or other. In pursuit of wisdom he is zealous; in resources, wonderfully fertile; a constant philosopher, an awesome enchanter and rhetorician, like Socrates.

Furthermore, the spirit of Eros stands in the gray area between ignorance and wisdom. Gods do not pursue wisdom the way Eros does, for the gods know everything already. Nor do the wholly ignorant seek wisdom; for this is the evil of ignorance, that people who are neither good nor wise remain satisfied, having no desire for virtues they do not know they need. Those who seek wisdom are those who find themselves somewhere between the wise and the foolish. Eros is one of those.

Thus Plato describes the character of Eros.

This is the spirit that comes and goes in us, as we fall in and out of love.

In the *Symposium,* Socrates describes his fateful meeting with Diotima of Mantineia, his instructress in the art of love. In the voice of this wise woman, Plato gives the account of the spirit of Eros I have summarized. But Socrates will not let Diotima stop with a mere description of the spirit. He wants to know more, just as we want to know more about Eros, how and why the spirit works in us.

She is going to tell us.

But first she reminds us of what she said before: Love is not beautiful—it is the *beloved* who is truly beautiful and good. Love is love of the beautiful. Now if we have got this firmly in mind, the great prophetess of Mantineia, in her long robes, will continue.

She tells us that those who love the beautiful and good desire to possess these; the possession of the good and beautiful makes us happy. Furthermore, and this is very important, no one is content to possess the good or the beautiful for just a little while. We desire the everlasting possession of the beautiful. This desire is universal in humanity, and takes many different forms.

And what are they doing, these creatures who show all this eagerness and heat that is called love? All animals, birds, and beasts fall into agony when love infects them, beginning with the desire for sexual union; for this, salmon leap the waterfalls, stags joust with their horns, and men have been known to fight duels and abandon thrones. Then, to this desire for union is added the care of offspring, for whom even the weakest parent will battle to the death against the strongest predators; for we will suffer anything in order to protect our children.

Why do we do these things?

"Well," says Diotima, the wise woman, "it is like this. The object we have in view is birth in beauty, whether of body or soul. All of us reach a certain age when we desire to procreate. The procreation must be in beauty and not in deformity. This procreation is the union of man and woman, and a divine thing; for conception and generation are an immortal principle in the mortal creature. Beauty presides over all birth in mind and body. This is why, when the time is ripe, and your thriving nature is full, you feel such a flutter and ecstasy about beauty whose approach promises an alleviation of those labor pains."

"For love is not, as you imagine, the love of the beautiful only," says the prophet lady.

"Then what is it?" I ask her, thinking of the honey-haired young woman I saw on the corner.

"The love of generation and of birth in beauty."

"Really?" I am suddenly embarrassed.

"Yes, indeed," she says. "Because, for us mortals, generation is as close as we can come to eternity and immortality. And if love is of the *everlasting* possession of the good, all of us will necessarily desire immortality together with the good: and so love is love of immortality."

This is one of the most remarkable features of the doctrine of love. We must not let this advice slip away from us before we have got a good, firm grip on it. For this is the lesson that will help us navigate the rough seas of desire.

A constant headache for anyone trying to understand love is the paradox of desire. You desire only what you lack—this is the nature of desire. You want breakfast because you have not eaten, and when you have had your eggs and bacon, you will no longer desire breakfast. If I am totally healthy, I cannot want health. So how can I desire my wife, if I already have her?

I want that beautiful woman in the miniskirt, but the instant I have her, I cannot desire her.

Now this is not simply a language problem, a playful mischief of words. When considered as a fundamental motive of human love, desire that fails becomes a frustrating, if not wholly devisive, principle. So worrisome is desire, in fact, that several Eastern religions strive to abolish desire altogether as a wicked delusion.

But we can find good practical help in the discussion of immortality. Again, we find wise advice in the husky voice of the sage Diotima.

We want good things to last forever; but, being mortal, we can go just so far in approaching the everlasting and the immortal, and then they escape us. The closest we can come to immortality is *generation*, because generation always leaves behind a new existence in place of the old. Babies are only one kind of generation. There are lots of other kinds—poetry, gardening, medicine. Even in the life of one man, we observe the succession or generation of selves between youth and age, as his body changes, hair, bone and flesh, and his soul develops its tempers and desires.

There is a law of succession which preserves all mortal things, not as exactly the same but by substitution. The old worn-out mortality leaves another new and similar existence behind. You see how different this is from the changeless immortality of a god, for whom there is no past or future. Being mortal, you are not one person forever; you are a series of people who follow each other. That is all the immortality we mortals can ever know.

One more time: When the wise lady talks about immortality, she does not mean Heaven, she means *generation*. And when she talks about generation, she does not mean making babies, or *just* babies, though babies are one fine way of generation. There are lots of other ways of generation: poetry, philosophy, governing, and gymnastics, whatever activity leads productively into the future. Love led me to books and Paul to engines and my sister to journalism. Eating your lunch might be considered a way of generation, if you are not the same exact person when you begin the meal as you are when you get up from the table. Every moment of everyone's life is potentially a moment of generation. Love links these moments. If Eros were not busy inspiring this continuous birth of self into self, we would have no continuity of personality, no connection of yesterday and today, no hope from today to tomorrow. A person would be much like an ox.

How does this help us to resolve the paradox of desire? How does it help me to live with my lust for that long-legged beauty in the miniskirt?

I understand now that what got me so excited is, quite frankly, my desire to regenerate physically in her beautiful body; after all, I know absolutely nothing else about her. Desire is the driving force of human love—and the person I most desire will be most illuminating in the long run, a woman I can desire again and again.

I also understand now that the erotic impulse demands more than a moment's satisfaction, being designed, as it was, for *permanent* possession of the beautiful. This would depend upon the young stranger and me establishing a *continuity* of harmonious selves, as in friendship. And we are not set up for that—at least, I am not.

Once upon a time I thought all I wanted was to embrace that beautiful woman for an hour or so. Now I see why we cannot be so easily satisfied. Eros, as we know him now, desires more, and more, and more. Each of us is busy generating selves to live beyond that ecstatic hour of sex. The future man in me, and the future woman in her, each has some new desire to be satisfied, and so on into eternity. Now that I have made eye contact with her and exchanged smiles, I shall go back to my work, and then home to my family whom I can love forever.

I did not learn these things from any book, not even a book as good as the *Symposium*.

The truth is, I was blessed in knowing good women, beginning with Annie Berman, my childhood friend. Annie and I encountered Eros at about the same time, and learned from comparing notes. We learned that those who grow up together, siblings almost, may see each other too clearly to flourish as lovers through the romantic adventure of young adulthood. In another time and place our parents might have arranged a marriage that would have worked out well for both families—it is easy for us to see that now, as adult friends.

But in the 1960s, marriage was not to be our destiny. We would have to fall in love with strangers.

V EROS AND THE AGE

Vivian Renka sat in the front row of my high school math class. With her long legs and neck, she was like a costly rose that might not open. She had a braid of dark hair with red highlights which sprang from the crown of her delicate head and flowed almost to her slender waist. Before class she would look over her shoulder at me, bemusedly, as if there were some joke on me that no one understood but Vivian.

I liked her anyway. Once class started, she sat straight as a duchess and looked strictly at the teacher or at her book, through horn-rimmed glasses. Her hand was always in the air first with the right answers. Her voice was musical. When the bell rang and Vivian got up, all the boys in class jostled to get behind her, because she had the most perfect dancer's legs they had ever seen.

By contemporary standards she was not outstandingly pretty, though she was certainly eye-catching. I was not sure what about her then was so engaging. Her nose was rather flat, which, taken together with the pigtail, made her seem almost oriental, if it had not been for the eyes—wide-set, cinnamon brown, and huge, with well-defined, arched eyebrows and long lashes. Her ears looked as if they belonged to two different people. Her mouth was small and looked compressed from her concentration in math class.

All of the boys looked at her; and not one of us could have known why, that what we were drawn toward was an ordinary-looking high school girl who in five years would be a world-class beauty. She would stop traffic.

Within a few weeks the math teacher discovered that Vivian had moved so far ahead of the rest of us that we would never catch up. It was dangerous to morale. So the girl with the long braid was transferred to a special math class designed to prepare five students for calculus by their senior year. Five students out of nine hundred in the entire class. Much later I would find out that math was not one of Vivian Renka's best subjects. She did not particularly like it.

Vivian gathered up her books and left for her special math class, and that was the last I remember seeing of her until the spring dance. I attended the prom with a hot date, a girl with whom I was sexually intoxicated.

Vivian had not been invited to attend the dance as anyone's date. She had agreed to come as our entertainment. It was a theme dance: The cafeteria had been dressed up for a Hawaiian luau, with palm trees and tons of sand. Hearing that Vivian was a dancer, some teenage entrepreneur had persuaded her to don a grass skirt and put on a little floor show, a hula review, as the climax to the Polynesian festivities.

Now Vivian had enormous dignity. But she also had a puckish sense of humor, and perhaps a semiconscious desire to change her image. This was *not* just a brainy girl who liked to sit at home on Saturday nights searching out new derivations for the quadratic formula. Vivian had social ambitions, and she particularly loved dancing.

So she agreed to perform for us.

And at a moment toward the end of the evening, the house lights dimmed. A spotlight shone on the doorway where Vivian glided in upon the loopy chords of a Hawaiian guitar. The transformation in her was total, electrifying. She had freed her hair from the stranglehold of the braid, so it flowed in dark waves around her face and bare shoulders. She had taken off her eyeglasses, put a little lipstick on the mouth that was not yet in full bloom, and drawn a bit of liner and shadow on the fantastic eyes, which needed no help whatsoever. Her dancer's body, which had been straining—first under the volcanic pressures of puberty and then in the tight fashions of the sixties—was now turned loose in full glory by the grass skirt and the patch of flowered poplin that was struggling to cover her breasts. She danced, and swayed, and everyone's eyes danced with her.

After that I do not think Vivian ever had much trouble getting dates. There was no immediate change in her style of dress or her dignified carriage. The great length of hair went back into the braid, and the braid got twisted into a hive on the top of her head in the style of the period. She did trade her glasses for contact lenses, which made a difference, because her eyes were spectacular. No, there was little change in Vivian's manner, but she had been seen, suddenly, in a way no one had imagined her before. She knew it. Men sensed this and right away wanted to touch her. I did, too.

During that year of high school, my romantic energies had been invested in an affair that could only be described as puppy love. The young lady was sexy and passionate in the extreme, and the two of us spent many nights groping and pawing at each other, and days sighing across hallways and classrooms, yearning for night. The two of us had enough libido to drive the power system of a small city—and this in the days when civilized fifteen-year-olds did not go "all the way." We went just as far as we could, whenever we could, exercising an ingenuity on the erotic frontiers that kept us constantly at the edge of madness, deprived of satisfaction. In fact, you might say that more thought was squandered upon having sex without having sex than was present in any other dimension of the affair. The young woman had an hourglass figure, sultry eyes and lips, and powerful maternal instincts. She was every high school boy's sexual fantasy, so I had to defend my position in the pantheon of her admirers. There were scenes of jealousy and anger, very primitive. I had not pursued the young woman for her mind, which was an efficient little engine as fifteen-year-old minds go, especially in pitting suitors against one another. But hers was not the sort of intellect to sustain my interest beyond her bedroom, if I ever got there.

So you see I was definitely ready for something richer when Vivian and I began to notice each other. This process was so gradual and subtle I cannot exactly reconstruct it. When we returned from summer vacation in our junior year, we found ourselves in the same classes, except for math class. We sat near each other in advanced-placement English and history. In that huge public high school only five boys got into this academic, fast-track program, to hold their own against twenty-five girls. So it is not remarkable Vivian noticed me. As for the girls, they had not been selected for their looks, and Vivian already stood out like a red poppy in a wheatfield.

We shared an interest in dramatics, and soon we got involved in theater productions together. I may have gone to her apartment the first time after driving her home from a play rehearsal.

I have difficulty remembering precisely what happened, because I seem to have been in a fog. Something was happening to me I did not quite understand. She seemed more in control of the process than I; she knew what must happen, what was transpiring between us long before I had any inkling. I was still involved, infatuated, with that girl who had the magnetic sexual charm, when Vivian and I began studying together. I may have thought I was still in love with that sultry temptress just as Vivian and I were becoming friends. But Vivian probably knew better. She sympathized with my adolescent, romantic melodramas, listening with good-humored interest without taking me too seriously. Did she know I was falling in love with her, inevitably, profoundly, and forever? Was that the meaning of the smile she sent me over her shoulder in math class, before we had even been introduced?

We were friends first, drawn together through admiration I like to think was mutual. I admired her quick insights, as we studied American literature and history. I prized these before I traced their expression in her somber concentration, her rippling laughter, and the perfect carriage of her head and shoulders. It was a striking combination of dignity and joy in her own good flesh, a dancer's grace. She was precociously magisterial as a director of high school plays, a born leader. Other students followed her direction unquestioningly, and promptly. The thing I admired about her most of all was that she had ambition, coupled with discipline. Gifted with a formidable intellect, she still reached beyond herself in every task she undertook. She had endless ambitions she would soon reveal to me in dreams and visions like my own.

V CRYSTALLIZATION

Vivian and I fell in love at a formative, highly impressionable stage of adulthood. Because of our dramatic influence upon each other's personality, our experience clearly illustrates a phenomenon known as "crystallization."

Stendhal observed that if you break off an ordinary twig and throw it into the salt water at the Salzburg mines, you will find the twig wonderfully transformed when you retrieve it the next day. The humble stick has been embroidered with glittering iridescent crystals. Just such a thing, says the author of *De l'amour,* happens to the likeness of your beloved when you fall in love. Little by little the real image of the man or woman, which entered your soul in the shape of an ordinary mortal, becomes built up with these imagined superstructures, wishful crystals that add to the mortal figure every possible perfection. Plato uses a more humble, homespun expression to describe the process—"winnowing." When you fall in love, Eros inspires you to "winnow out" your beloved's perfections, to separate what is worthy to be loved from what is not.

I believe this crystallization is part of Love's course of instruction, which is preparing us for ever and ever higher sentiments. When I first met Vivian, she was an ordinary girl with large brown eyes and a knack for mathematics and hulas. By the time Eros had been working on us for two years or so, she had become, to my mind, almost a goddess. Crystallization had done such a thorough job of highlighting her virtues I could no longer mistake the divinity in Vivian—and once I had seen what was divine, I could never again be wholly content to love merely the mortal. On her part, she met a rather self-satisfied boy who played football passably, was contemptuous of his popularity, and had inchoate ambitions. Her love imagined me a young hero destined for greatness, a rare soul trapped in the suffocating role of a 1960s high school student.

The second or third time I drove Vivian home from our play rehearsal, she invited me to come inside for a glass of iced tea. We talked of our ambitions. She wanted to go to Swarthmore College, the exclusive school on the Main Line of Philadelphia. In those days it was nearly impossible for a woman from our gigantic public high school system to get into such a college. The pride of the senior class the year ahead of us had been admitted to the super-exclusive college, and you would think she had ascended into Heaven, the way teachers spoke of her in hushed tones, rolling their eyes. Vivian wanted to follow her footsteps through the ivied gates of Swarthmore.

I wanted to go to Harvard, of course, and become President or the greatest playwright since Eugene O'Neill, whichever came first: These were quixotic ambitions, especially Harvard. Our middle-class suburban public school of three thousand souls had not gotten a single graduate into Harvard, Yale, or Princeton in twenty years; everyone who applied was rejected, whereas none of us had ever been formally denied the presidency.

No one we knew would waste time applying to Harvard, except me. Most of us would go to the state university, or to work for our parents, or straight into wedlock. But I was bound for the Ivy League. I never gave a thought to being rejected, though I would be, while Vivian, who really would go to Swarthmore, doubted it until the day she got her acceptance.

So we talked until late at night. As I left, she shook my hand with a grip like a lumberjack's. I complimented her on her hands, which were perfectly formed.

The second or third time we had tea together in her living room, my praise of her long hair mixed with teasing about the braid being twisted eternally in the hive on top of her head. I said the dark mass was probably glued there, or petrified; that she never let it down even to sleep, could not let it down even if she tried.

So she would show me, smiling. One foot tucked under her lovely seat, just next to me on the couch, Vivian raised her hands, plunged her fingers into the dark hair, and began removing, one by one, what seemed like a hundred pins that held the braid coiled, setting the pins on the glass surface of the coffee table in front of us. When the braid was free, Vivian swung it around her right shoulder, smoothing the length with one hand and then the other. While looking at me with wide eyes that were more bold than fearful, she removed the gold-tipped thong that bound the braid, and deftly unraveled it. She shook the hair back over her head while running her long fingers through it, and when Vivian looked as if she was peering out at me from under a dark waterfall, her mouth half open, I kissed her.

And when the two of us had caught our breath, we kissed again, as the room spun around us. I do not think Vivian had ever kissed a man this way before, and she seemed eager to learn while making up for lost time. We kissed again and again, and then it was way past time for me to leave. I kissed my way out the door, stumbled down the stairs of her apartment building into the dark, and nearly wrecked the car on my way home.

We were not yet seventeen, and Vivian was not fully grown. That is, she had some growing to do, though she had attained her full height, half a head shorter than my six feet.

I had a friend who was the high school yearbook photographer. He had just finished shooting a roll of film of the high school dance company, of which Vivian was a principal dancer.

My friend was avid to share with me some photographs of Vivian leaping, in her leotard and tights. They were truly a joy to behold. The woman, he observed, was perfectly, voluptuously finished from the waist down, a veritable Venus de Milo. As for the rest of her, she was an ethereal nymph, a perfect intersection of erotic body and spirit—heaven above and rich earth below. My friend bobbed his thick eyebrows.

Well, this is the image that Eros worked its magic upon. For a long time neither of us wanted to kiss anyone else. We spent a lot of time practicing the art, until we thought we were quite good at it. I do not know where we found the time, as serious as we were about our schoolwork. But the kissing made time for itself, and some highly creative and accelerated petting followed.

We went dancing whenever we could, and when the music of the Rolling Stones or Smokey Robinson got us good and worked up, we would go outside and kiss under the stars, or speed home where in stolen privacy we could flirt with the goal of our desires. In the two and a half years from the time of our first kiss until Vivian and I abandoned ourselves to the ecstatic pleasures of Eros, I cannot remember a moment when she ever raised a hand to check my advances, the two of us were so certain of our terrain. What was hers was mine, she had decided, and I knew this without her having to tell me. When at last we would go to bed together, both virgins, we marveled at the touch of each other's flesh, how it could be so thrilling, my pale skin upon her dark skin, at the same time feeling miraculously as if we were one flesh. What was mine was hers, and that included a sacral appreciation of her wishes, her desires.

She explained to me, when we had been dating for several months, that she had two major ambitions. She wanted to be with me forever, to marry and have a family, anywhere but here. Her other ambition was Swarthmore, which would deliver her out of the dreary world of her family, as well as the dullness of lower-middle-class suburbia to which she had been assigned.

Her family was indeed sad. Their little apartment was pervaded with an Old World melancholy. Vivian's mother had died giving birth to her third child when Vivian, the eldest, was eleven. Her father, an elegant, urbane Frenchman, had married late and would never remarry. His work as a diplomatic translator kept him away in Europe and South America for ten months of the year. Mr. Renka wrote long beautiful letters which Vivian treasured, with all their exotic and gilded details.

During his long absences Mr. Renka entrusted the care of his daughters and son to his older sister Maude, who must have been in her seventies when I knew her. She was a tall and lethargic lady so afflicted with emphysema there seemed to be a constant whistling, like a tiny teakettle, from the back bedroom where Maude lay among piles of remnants. From them she fashioned, with an antique charm, the shirts and dresses for the three children.

The family had an air of exiled royalty. Maude was old but seemed older, as if she mourned the passing of a golden age she had only dreamed or glimpsed without entirely possessing. During the forties and early fifties she had lived abroad, under vague domestic circumstances, in Italy. Her stories always recounted how sumptuously and respectfully she had been treated in Milan or Rome or Paris on her visits there, how well she had been wined and dined and lodged. At the dinner table Aunt Maude presided, as from a distinguished height, while Vivian and her brother Louis served the meal. Louis was thin, pale, and plain, utterly spectral. By the time I met Vivian, Louis was in his early teens, but his shoulders were not broad enough to bear the burdens of the surrogate "man of the house." So Vivian, in effect, became both father and mother to Louis and her little sister, Miriam, who looked like Louis in miniature but with thick eyeglasses. At seven she had sought refuge in the silent fortress of storybooks, which had to be taken from Miriam by force before she would eat or go to bed.

In this gloomy atmosphere, the twilight of an aristocracy overbred to the edge of extinction, Vivian shone like a final ray of sunlight. She literally danced around that apartment, laughing, lifting everyone's spirits and holding them up to the light like scarecrows. She had energy enough for five people when she was a teenager. But by the time I met her, Vivian's melancholy family had, I believe, already consumed the dividends of the bright sister's fund of happiness; they had already begun to eat into the young woman's emotional capital.

And it was not only affection and entertainment they needed. Vivian's Aunt Maude scarcely had strength to direct the household. She relied heavily upon Vivian to do the cleaning, shopping, and cooking. Vivian often could not get to her homework until early morning.

She may have thought our love had arrived just in time to save her, whether or not she would admit this to herself. Our kissing almost seemed to breathe life into her body, and a remarkable thing happened.

With each night of kissing, she grew more beautiful. Her lips grew full and red, so she never needed lipstick; the flat nose took a strong and graceful shape; most remarkable, in a period of one year of kissing, the roundness of the upper half of the body that I had studied in photographs grew to rival the curves below her waist. The shoulders broadened, her breasts swelled until they stretched the stitches of her wool sweaters. It was as if she had filled out to fit my erotic ideal. And the sixties encouraged her to show it off. She wore miniskirts, and frocks that amounted to no more than long shirts, in the summer, and brief halters—clothing that was more provocative than straight nudity. Men would cling to lampposts and sigh as she walked by.

You may say the development of Vivian's figure was genetically determined, and our love had no hand in it. But I am not so certain. The love between young people is a colossal thing, always to be respected and never to be underestimated. It makes a perfect subject for the study of crystallization, because in cases like ours the lovers begin to *mirror* each other's ideal. When I met Vivian, she was a wise and ethereal fairy with the legs of a chorus girl. Beginning with those fantastic legs, I built upon their foundation, crystal by crystal, a whole erotic ideal, a complete Venus. And Vivian brought this into being so quickly, the ideal vaporized in the fire of the living woman. She was beautiful beyond anything I could have imagined.

The year after we graduated from high school, she got a summer job in a department store in downtown Washington, D.C., selling ladies' fashions. The style editor of the *Washington Post* showed up one afternoon to cover a "trunk show" at the store, and the aisles were overrun with high fashion models. But all the photographers kept turning, phototropically, toward Vivian, as if this salesclerk were the only woman in the vicinity.

The next morning when we opened the newspaper, there was Vivian on the front page of the Style section of the *Washington Post* showing off a Chanel blouse.

This was the beginning and the end of her modeling career. She would soon be off to Swarthmore College to study Italian, philosophy, and choreography. Like other women who become beautiful after an undistinguished adolescence, Vivian never developed vanity enough for a career as a professional beauty. And she was so bright—all of that make-up, and hair styling, and standing around like a store-window dummy would have bored her to death. She would become the opposite of a fashion model: a dancer.

For Vivian the process of crystallization did not so much involve my physical person. She found me attractive enough, surely, and perhaps her love lent my figure an extra "glow." She definitely acted as if she desired me more than any woman I had ever known before. But Vivian saw in me, she said, the seeds of certain virtues, intellectual and moral virtues, which soon flowered richly in her imagination, when no one else could divine them. She would never worship me, but she would worship the divine in me. She saw me as great, and gifted, and good when I was not any of these things but more of a muddle of opinions and ambitions. Her image of me was so admirable I could not resist it—in fact, I would strive to grow into her spiritual ideal, just as she had filled out my vision of erotic perfection.

She is a woman of sacred principles, highly evolved, the sort of woman whose prayers in earlier times might have delivered entire cities from the plague. Her power to love, at that tender age, overwhelmed mine, no matter how much I tried to love her. And not only did she have this innate power, but her crippled family had forced upon Vivian a habit of sacrifice, upon which all of them had become dependent. As her emotional and physical resources seemed endless to her family, so her strength began to seem infinite to Vivian. Another woman might have dreamed someone would deliver her from that dying family by strengthening her in love, fathering her children, by making a great success and then bankrolling all of them. Not Vivian. For her, selfishness was as unthinkable as cruelty. She would love me unselfishly. Vivian would love me in the same way she had learned to love her family, but with the full power of a mature woman . . .

Her passion can only be described as heroic. I do not take credit for inspiring it, any more than she takes credit for my love for her. It was Ortega's centrifuge at work on Plato's daemon: when two people love as Vivian and I loved, there is feedback, and the passion is subject to what she and I proudly called "the law of augmenting returns," a dizzying acceleration.

She had the gift of emptying herself entirely into the passion. And between play rehearsal, dance class, housekeeping for her mother, making love with me, and burning the midnight oil in order to get into Swarthmore College, Vivian averaged maybe four hours of sleep a night. She lived on coffee and salads during her senior year in high school. I did all I could to help her, including housekeeping. I chided her for the dark circles under her eyes, and begged her to give something up, anything but me. Laughing, she said I would be the last to go. Except for the dark circles under her eyes, she looked to be in perfect health, and energetic enough to serve everybody and everything. Love was our food and fuel.

What was she giving me?

During that time in my life, when I could not figure out who I would become, Vivian had a clear vision of my future. I came to her with rambling descriptions of my unearthly ambitions, my longing and doubts, and she helped me to sift through the rubbish, keeping what was of value that truly belonged to me. This sifting transpired in hundreds of hours of conversation in which the flow passed always from me to her, then back to me *through* her, distilled and purified. She knew who *she* was, no doubt, and needed no reciprocal consideration; at least that was my impression at the time.

In the class of nine hundred high school seniors, she graduated fifth and I was seventh. We lifted our glasses of champagne with a toast to ourselves, for we had done it together. Before she took off for Swarthmore, and I for college five hundred miles west, we made a firm agreement in one another's arms. We would not allow the distance to diminish our passion.

And in four years, God willing, we would resume our life together.

But Vivian grew wistful, momentarily, in one such conversation, as if she had a doubt even her magnificent faith could not silence. She looked over my shoulder as we sipped at our wine in a restaurant. The waiter kept his distance. When I pressed her to tell me what was troubling her, Vivian told me she had felt, oddly, as if she were disappearing. It was like a sudden chill. And when I asked her what she meant by that, she laughed, forcibly, and said that, of course, some day she *would* disappear. So would all of us. Yet her words held a tone of personal foreboding.

She had the gift of saints and martyrs: She could deny her mortal flesh and even her ego for the advancement of spirit. In college study, and later in the discipline of the dance studio, she would refine her own spirit beyond anything I am likely to achieve in this life. Our lovemaking was, from the first, a voluptuous sacrament. We made love by candlelight, daylight, or no light at all—in 1969 our lovemaking was the closest thing we had to a religion.

She would keep her part of our bargain. I have preserved a thousand of her letters, written from 1966 to 1973 from Swarthmore, Rome, and then from Chicago where she went to pursue her dance career after college. They are amazing letters. They have two major themes: the transcendent beauty of our love for each other, and the absolute certainty that I must become the man she dreamed, as great and gifted, as loyal and good.

I owe her a great deal. It was my fortune to catch her on the way up, during a phase of physical eroticism, when our bodies could meet, before the woman became a transparent flame and passed me forever. In college what had begun as a generative passion began to consume her. We had thought that once she arrived at Swarthmore, her destination, then she could relax and begin to enjoy her life. But the challenges of that place were beyond anything that had tempted her in our poor suburban high school. She became austere and uncompromising in her efforts to meet tantalizing goals—academic, artistic, and personal goals—while still pursuing a passionate affair with me long distance, even from Rome, where she had gone to study in her junior year. Alternating with the periods of furious activity came days of sadness. I disappointed her terribly. She chain-smoked and consumed frightening amounts of coffee. In her early twenties, she began to lose weight.

I disappointed Vivian and myself by falling in love with someone else, though I never thought it would happen. Caught between old and new love, I betrayed both women and myself. Vivian was disappearing, just as she said she would. The phone calls from Rome were frantic, mournful, and expensive. She did not need a transatlantic monitor to see that I was involved with another woman; Vivian had become so finely tuned she could see any distance and back and forth in time.

I did not love her any less. And, indeed, I would never love her any less. So it became impossible, when Vivian returned the next year, for me to continue my relationship with Madeline Carter, the woman I had come to love while Vivian was in Europe. And later it was impossible for me to tell Vivian that we would never marry. Yet she knew it.

She was devoted to me, as I was to her, but Vivian was no fool. The summer after college graduation, she came to collect. I told her I was not ready to be married. I told her I had some traveling and writing to do. She began to weep, silently, and I did not know how to comfort her. I had failed her, and she was mourning for both of us. When she finally regained her composure, Vivian told me I had two years to make up my mind, two years exactly.

I did not take her altogether seriously. During those years of wandering, after college, I was casually involved with several different women. When I could get to Chicago, I would stay with Vivian, who had gone there to study dance and starve herself down to skin, bones, and devotion. Her huge eyes glowed in her head like blazing coals. Our lovemaking was passionate to the point of violence, as if she would tear away the very flesh that separated our two souls. Or perhaps she was struggling to free us from each other.

At the end of the allotted grace period, I called to come and see her, and she told me, without expression, that my time was up. I told her she must be kidding.

Laughing, I hung up the phone and caught the next train to Chicago. From the station, I called Vivian, who politely repeated what she had told me from long distance. I took a cab to her apartment building, mounted the four flights of stairs, and rang her bell. She would not let me in the door.

It should be clear without comment why such a relationship does not end in a successful marriage. Though our attachment had elements of a good marriage—strong erotic sentiment, a firm base of friendship; yet it lacked balance. She emptied herself entirely into her love for me. I could never love Vivian anywhere near as much as she loved me, so I would be constantly in debt to her. She was so far advanced in the progress from mortal body to imperishable ether, that she might be satisfied in a marriage only with someone equally evolved, a spiritual master. And if she had not found such a man, I believe she might have ended her days in solitude. She is happily married to a man I greatly esteem and am proud to call my friend.

But I have not dwelt at such length on this chapter of my life merely to illustrate the effects of crystallization or the dangers of spiritual disparity in a couple. The story has a broader meaning. Vivian is typical of her generation in some significant ways. With Vivian's permission, I will use the dancer's figure as the heroine of a ballet, the dance-drama of our midcentury. She will be the principal ballerina; and the entire generation of the 1960s, those who were young in the 1960s, we are the *corps de ballet* who mirror the ballerina's movements.

The dance-drama begins in the 1940s, as a dance of death. As the curtain goes up, Death, the skull-head leering out of his hooded cape, stands triumphant on the stage. The grim reaper has just herded six million Jews, blacks, and homosexuals into the gas chambers, before presiding over the orderly departure of several hundred thousand Japanese souls upon the detonation of atom bombs. Death is delighted. Eros, who looks like young Socrates, shakes his head sadly in the shadows upstage. Then comes an overture of soft romantic crooning by Bing Crosby and Frank Sinatra, to which the grim reaper dances a stiff-legged fox trot before the proscenium. The *corps de ballet* of young people is bored to sleep by the music.

Then we hear static on the sound system before the drumbeat of Buddy Holly's band, the Crickets. This is the birth of rock-and-roll, the true music of Eros. Buddy is singing "That'll Be the Day"; and as the vibrations play upon his ribcage, Death begins to boogie and truck and buck. He drops a bone here and a bone there in his enthusiasm. Then Elvis is heard singing "Don't Be Cruel," and Death falls apart altogether, a pile of bones twitching on the stage.

At this point we get an interlude of James Brown, Smokey Robinson and the whole gang at Motown, representing the transition from the fifties to the sixties. Eros slides downstage strutting like Mick Jagger while Vivian enters in a trance, leading the *corps de ballet*.

At first the prima ballerina looks starved, ethereal, a pure spirit with no physical desire but a yearning for what is good and essentially beautiful. As she watches Eros move and he beckons to her seductively, the girl seems to put on flesh. She begins to dance fluidly and then voluptuously, inspired by the music of carnal love. And, of course, all of us do the same, following her movements.

We cannot resist the drumbeat. This rock-and-roll is truly music to raise the dead—perhaps it may even raise the ten million who met their untimely deaths in the 1940s, when Eros was out to lunch. We shake and jump and dance to the music of Chuck Berry, the Beatles, and the Rolling Stones, and the dancing is an incitement to lovemaking; indeed, it is a kind of lovemaking in itself.

We move from dancing to making love, and this is more than a mating game. We make love, an entire generation, as no generation has ever made love, more times and with more different partners. We have antibiotics to prevent disease, and birth control to prevent unwanted pregnancy, so we make love to anyone we desire, in open meadows, in shadows or broad daylight of city streets and rooftops, on the village green, carelessly, defiantly, on television, anywhere the spirit of Eros moves us. Is this just another medieval dance of death, a manic blowout in anticipation of Doomsday? No. It is a ten-year revival meeting coast-to-coast. This generation re-invented the concept of youth for the benefit of a world that seemed to have given up on the idea of living, to rescue humanity that had set its weary sights on the graveyard. The lifeline was love.

LOVE AT FIRST SIGHT

There is one thing about Cupid that is worth keeping as a figure of speech: his weaponry.

The suddenness, the unexpectedness of love at first sight, and the keenness of the sensation in one's breast resemble the imagined progress of an arrow wound that festers, spreading its venom to all parts of the body. The arrow has been treated with a magic potion that enchants the victim. Think of the arrow as coming *from* the beloved, inadvertently: the chance arrow that comes from my beloved pierces me, and out of the opening my love flows toward her in a steady stream.

This has happened to me twice. Curiously, the two women had been close friends and classmates in prep school. After I had known her for several years, the first woman introduced me to the second, who eventually became my wife and the mother of my children. People's lives are full of strange co-incidences. But this is surely one of the weirdest in my own life, given that erotic era of the 1960s and my own restlessness and mobility. There was a vast field of potential partners. That I should be so deeply affected by two women who grew up together would seem to suggest a lack of adventurousness on my part, or some kind of conspiracy on theirs. Nothing could be further from the truth. The two women are totally different physical and personality types, and they had no intention of dividing my romantic interests between them.

I was a serious student. I chose a small all-male college in rural Ohio in the hope of minimizing the distractions of a hectic era of sex, drugs, and rock-and-roll.

I was so lost in my studies as a freshman that I could not tell one day from another, and on a Saturday night when the rest of the students had begun celebrating the weekend, I was huddled in my stall in the library, studying Kant's *Critique of Aesthetic Judgment*.

One friend grabbed me by the right arm, another by my left, and the next thing I knew I was airborne, on my way to the fraternity party where I would meet Madeline Carter.

As college parties go, this was a gentle one, even sedate. There was soft folk music strumming on the sound system, and people were standing around with cups of beer in their hands, in small groups, talking. Women were in the room: students' dates from women's colleges nearby or faraway, girls from the town, faculty wives.

I was not much interested in women that evening. Vivian,

my high school sweetheart, had matriculated at Swarthmore, seven hours away by car. I would burn up the highway every few weeks to see her, or she would fly in from Philadelphia to see me. We wrote passionate letters back and forth, talked on the phone once a week, and enjoyed our mutual longing. It seemed like a natural part of the rigor of our education, the pure life of the cloister. I walked into the fraternity party like a mole into daylight.

Madeline Carter was at the far end of the room, listening, as few people in this world can listen, while some unshaven sophomore explained to her his reason for living. I suppose that is what he was explaining. It matters only that he thought the topic was important, and Madeline would not let him think otherwise for a moment.

She was wearing a deep-red cape, which was exactly the same color as her hair, which was dazzling with her light green eyes. Her hair, in the manner of the late 1960s, was long and straight, flowing with its fiery highlights down her back but pinned back from her face to show the strong outline of her cheekbones and chin. She wore gold-rimmed granny glasses, which made her look a bit severe. Madeline had a streak of cynicism in her late teens, but this did not compromise her support of the young student as she listened to him, nodding, with her head tilting slightly to one side, her arms crossed. Rather, the cynicism lent credibility: If *she* believed him, his opinion must be worthy beyond any doubt.

She turned away from him briefly to look at me. The eyes were extraordinary, at once dreamy and all-seeing. I felt I was sinking right into her, and her lips parted just slightly, suggesting she had seen something similar in my glance. I watched her take a deep breath and, as if by an act of intense will, look away again. I moved toward her. She politely disengaged herself from the conversation she had been having, and gave me her full attention, which was awesome.

If I was conscious of anything at the time, it was of enormous power and capacity in this woman, all visible in the windows of her eyes. And I thought that somehow what I was seeing in there was part of myself. There was a unique blend of masculine force and feminine sympathy. Years later we would talk about that moment of meeting, what it had meant to each of us. I think she felt as strongly as I did, and the incident must have been terribly confusing to her. She already had a boyfriend, a young pianist with a promising career. He was in the room somewhere. I don't remember meeting him.

Madeline was never a woman to be stunned out of action or beyond words. She sounded me out, probably in the same way she had engaged my bearded predecessor in conversation, and listened to me with the same intensity as I told her of my dreams, to be a philosopher, a writer, a teacher. Her father was the dean of a neighboring college, and Madeline studied philosophy there, and was an amateur violinist; she would be leaving school soon to travel with the young pianist and perform in a trio in the East, and then if things worked out, perhaps in Europe.

Things did not work out, with the young pianist or with the whole trio, I was never quite sure which. But six months later Madeline was back home to live with her parents and her six sisters. By then I was a college junior, Vivian had flown to Italy for a year of study at the University of Rome, and Madeline and I were free to pick up where we had left off at the party in 1966.

Where exactly had we left off? As I left the party and walked alone under the October stars, Madeline's beautiful face haunted me. It was love at first sight. I felt certain this woman would become a significant figure in my life. I might have considered pursuing her in spite of her pianist, but something in the young woman's manner discouraged this. She was not the sort of person to be distracted from one serious affection by another, no matter how alluring; she was not the sort of woman to end an affair by beginning a new one. As for me, I was already involved with a woman I had loved since high school, whom I dreamed of marrying. So neither Madeline nor I was ready to begin a serious affair. But I felt certain our time would come.

What gives people such notions? The idea that two people are "meant for each other" probably goes back to a funny speech in the *Symposium*. Aristophanes explains to the gang at the all-night party that once upon a time, before men and women had their separate bodies, the human creature was a man-woman, with four arms, four legs, and so on. The man-woman was in constant ecstasy, and altogether too pleased with itself, until God with lightning bolts split the whole race of men-women into their separate halves. Ever since this day of trauma, each man and woman has searched for his or her other half, hoping to regain primordial ecstasy by being reunited with that other half, in perfect love.

I must have suspected that Madeline was my better half.

In college I read a book Goethe published in 1809, called *The Elective Affinities*. *Elective affinities* is an old term from chemistry. If you mix certain compounds, their component elements "change partners," so to speak. This is probably a source of our use of the word *chemistry* to describe the excitement between lovers. In Goethe's novel, dashing Edward and gentle Charlotte are happily married. Then Charlotte's niece, the lovely, mystical Ottilie, comes to visit their estate. Edward takes one look at little Ottilie and falls in love with her, and she with him. Charlotte, practical Charlotte, takes comfort in the company of an older man, a sea captain who also happens to be their house guest. It is a swinging party. The marriage falls apart, as each partner discovers his or her perfect soul mate.

The idea of elective affinities has come to refer to a romantic ideal, sometimes called the "romantic fallacy" by those who wish to discourage it. The theory is, in a nutshell, that somewhere out there, among the several billions of people alive during your lifetime on this planet, you may find the one person for whom you are the perfect mate. There is only one of them, and one of you. If you find that person, you will both know it, and nothing but death can separate you. The astrologers call such couples "astral twins" because their fates are ordained by the stars. Astrologers do not pretend to have the power to discover or ascertain whether two people are astral twins. But the best astrologers claim to calculate the likelihood of compatibility. In some cultures no couple may marry without a green light from the astrologer, so powerful is this belief in romantic destiny.

This ideal of perfect lovers, or astral twins, is extremely dangerous. The likelihood of its being true makes the idea even more tantalizing, persistent, and dangerous. It makes perfect mathematical sense that if human nature is infinitely various, and there are seven billion people in the world, only one of them can possibly be the perfect person for you. But who has time enough to find out? So you marry the person you love the most, and live with him or her for ten years. Suppose that *then* you meet your astral twin? What do you do? Suppose you meet someone who just *might* be your ideal lover? Do you pack up and move out? If you believe what Aristophanes told us at the all-night party, that only being united with your proper half can make you truly happy, you bet your life you would move out.

But this is a big world, with seven billion people. And if you are truly serious about the ideal, you may never stop looking. There is no end to this, no end to the frustration and suffering that follows the romantic ideal, true or not. The only people who can live sanely in the light of such an ideal are people who have realized it, the astral lovers. And can any of us be sure before we are dead? I know a happy couple who met in high school, and married at age twenty-one, thirty years ago. They were convinced then that they were meant for each other, and nothing but death would ever part them. I believe they were right. I have spent a lot of time in the company of these two lovers, and their children, and the couple is so perfectly tuned that at times the harmony between them seems nearly audible, like a humming of bees, even when they are arguing. Yet if anything could come between these lovers, it might be the further pursuit of the romantic ideal they believe first united them.

When I fell in love with Madeline Carter at first sight twenty years ago, I believed in our destiny together. I did not know how, but I knew that my future would depend upon her.

When Madeline returned to the little college town in the autumn of my junior year, we found each other at once. I sought her out as soon as I heard she had returned. We took a walk in a swirl of red maple leaves, and I told her what had happened to me at the party two years ago, when I had first met her. She remembered our meeting, and that she had put it out of her mind. And so much had happened since. Madeline told me about her tour with the musicians, and her affair with the young pianist. Though she had been unsure of the depths of his commitment, she had clung to him with a fury that marks first love, not knowing the love was half desperation, the adolescent fear that perhaps no man would ever love her enough.

I tried to assure Madeline that I would love her as she deserved to be loved, and in the true spirit of the 1960s, we became lovers without further ceremony or preamble.

And when we were not making love, we would be talking. I had never met a woman who conversed like Madeline, who had so many ideas and such a passion for communicating them clearly. It did not take me long to realize that this is what I had seen in her eyes—intellectual power and capacity, rather than any purely physical power of regeneration. Other women had sex appeal, and I was all for it. Vivian had it, and she had great intelligence as well, and listened resonantly. But Madeline not only listened; she gave as much as she received, so as to make a virtue of my listening.

She had two great themes: theology and the women's movement. In her quiet, rational way, Madeline Carter was one of the philosophical revolutionaries of the late 1960s. Her father, an academic dean who taught philosophy, had fathered seven daughters. Madeline suspected him of having wanted a son. As the eldest daughter, and the most intellectual, she would challenge him as a son might.

A tall, powerful man with a booming voice, Dean Harold Carter was a man of steadfast principles, great courage, and patience. He was a tireless peacemaker during the academic rebellions that climaxed at Kent State. A prodigy of youthfulness, at fifty the dean looked half his wife's age. I liked his courage and humor, and so did his daughters, who nevertheless resented what they perceived in him as male condescension.

I thought his manner was simply an unconscious strategy, given his family structure, a necessary defense of a man constantly outnumbered by women. He looked upon my courtship of his daughter with the good humor of a man of the world who has seen worse suitors, coming and going. When I showed an interest in philosophy, particularly the writings of Hume, the dean conversed with me as an equal and accepted me into the household practically as a family member. We became close friends, and remained friends until he died.

Madeline had her father's intellectual power and her mother's earthy humor, intuition, and common sense. Not that Mrs. Carter was a slouch in the realm of ideas—she could hold her own with any philosopher. Mrs. Carter was an attractive, slender attorney, with a low voice that was wry one moment and dreamy the next. She loved to read and quote from the poems of T. S. Eliot, while musing upon the fate of her seven daughters. Mrs. Carter had less vanity than any woman I have ever known—it seemed like a form of confidence almost, or fatalism, the way her gray hair flopped in her face, moplike, and she would toss a handful out of the way so she could fix me with a clear blue eye and say, "I *think* the girls would do better to sleep at *night,* don't *you?*"

I pretended not to have an opinion. Her casual clothing might have come from the church rummage sale; and I always remember her wearing carpet slippers and a wrinkled apron, though actually she may not have owned one. She was the kind of person in whom you could confide almost anything. And in case you did not, she had such great intuitive powers she would know pretty much what was on your mind anyway. She could answer the most delicate human questions. Some days I would come to call on Madeline and, finding her not at home, would sit with Mrs. Carter, drinking pots of coffee and solving the world's problems. She had a remarkable combination of zany humor and common sense.

Madeline got the best qualities of both parents, plus a degree of physical beauty that was beyond either of them.

That autumn she got a job as a nurse's aide, to make a little money and to prepare to become a nurse herself. That was her ambition then. When she was done with her schoolwork and I was finished with my studies, we would meet as soon as possible, to talk and make love. We slept very little the first months we were together.

I knew nothing about Christianity, though my mother, like Madeline, was Christian. I thought Christians were mostly sentimental, foggy-headed do-gooders and missionaries who believed in a fire-and-brimstone Hell and a Heaven of harps and angels. I thought Christians groveled before the altar of their bleeding Christ and gloried, above all, in their groveling and humility. But Madeline knew her religion from the inside out, and began to explain to me the fundamentals, the variations, the subtleties of Christian theology. She explained the concept of "service," using her parents as examples. This moved me, for I had grown up in a family with little social conscience. My father regarded the family as an armed camp, a defense against the world; while these amazing, naïve Christians trusted the potential of the whole community to behave like one happy family. They believed this and lived by their belief. And Madeline explained to me the concept of grace (which has its subtler counterpart in Judaism): the notion that God is essentially merciful, and Christ is an instrument of divine mercy.

She was not trying to convert me, for her own faith was highly speculative and broadminded; she only wanted to open my eyes to a range of possibilities. She was equally curious about my Judaism and my philosophical adventures.

But when we came to the subject of the women's movement, Madeline's tone would change. There was less room for controversy in a state of warfare. A war was going on between men and women, a war more divisive in its way than Vietnam; for all righteous hippies denounced our role in Southeast Asia, while half the American population, the men, were denying they had enslaved the other half, the nation's women.

In the war between the sexes, I would have to be either with Madeline or against her. I wanted to be with her in all things, because I loved her. So I listened carefully as she explained to me how men, from the dawn of time, had deprived women of their freedom to move, think, and grow; how from the moment a child is born, society assigns the child a role according to its sex; and how women are raised to be subservient, passive, and inferior to men. She explained that while woman's status had improved since the Dark Ages and shown creditable advances in the Renaissance and the twentieth century, sexual inequality before the law—in the marketplace, the classroom, and household—was still extreme and affronted the dignity of women *and* men.

Now you know exactly what sort of family I came from. It was openly patriarchal. My father came home with the money.

When he spoke, everybody listened and did what he told them to do, right away. Madeline's family was subtler patriarchy, a kind of limited patriarchy that sometimes looked almost like a democracy. The dean knew how things ought to be, and would talk it over with you logically if you liked, so as to leave no doubt in your mind about how things ought to turn out. He only told people what they must do when they were not already doing it of their own volition. Then they did what he told them to do, right away. As he was the only man in the house, this did look an awful lot like sexism, to the women.

If I had been less in love with Madeline, I would not have listened to her, and she would never have convinced me that I was a hopeless, unregenerate sexist. I had come from a family and social stratum where "sexism" was so much a way of life it never occurred to me sexism was unnatural, unhealthy, wicked, and contemptible. No one among my family or friends ever grumbled about it. Vivian, the central love interest of my high school years, offered no open challenge to the status quo. Though I disliked my father's tyranny over my mother, my need to behave differently from my father came from some inner sense of justice, not from any woman I had ever met—until Madeline. So I listened to her.

I listened carefully, and agreed with almost everything she said: that women had gotten a raw deal throughout history; and there were still gross and more subtle forms of discrimination between the sexes, domination and humiliation of women which must end, by consciousness raising and by legislation outrageously overdue. I assented to all she said, except for one point. This was only one point, but it drove her batty.

Madeline insisted that men and women, man and woman, are the same at birth. As much as I loved her, this proposition defied my sense of logic and anatomical reality, and I could not bring myself to assent to it. I tried. I turned it over and over in my mind. Everything else Madeline said made sense, so I figured that if I studied the proposition long enough, this would come clear as well—but it never did. I balked. She told me this was the very heart of the problem! She fumed. As long as men and women were perceived as different, men would use the distinction as an excuse for exploitation; the difference would be viewed in terms of men's superiority in strength, speed, and large-motor coordination, if not in their superior logical faculties. It just was not fair. I suggested that the distinction might be regarded merely in terms of sensibility, but she was not having any of that. She turned a deaf ear to me and threw up her hands in exasperation.

But this was our only point of disagreement, a bit of sand in the gears of an otherwise smooth-running, well-lubricated engine of dialogue. We talked, we sympathized and learned from each other, and there was never an argument that would not dissolve in laughter or lovemaking. I remember that year of college in Madeline's company as one of the most purely joyful in my life, and there were times when we thought it must never end. I took her to meet my mother and my grandparents on the Eastern Shore of Maryland. She charmed everyone in my family.

We talked of marriage, but neither of us was ready. Vivian returned from Rome, and I felt myself drawn back to her by a force I could not properly explain to Madeline or myself. For the next year I was torn between these two women who represented my past and my future. Too young to know my own mind or heart, I could not honor my commitment to either woman and remained stalled painfully between them. All of us paid a certain price for our freedom in the sixties.

It would be commendable if we could "tune up" the doctrine of love to perfect pitch, preparing it and ourselves for the twenty-first century. No generation has ever been so well prepared.

My grandfather was a man of the world. He lived adventurously, loved deeply, and delighted in sharing his experiences with his grandson. What he declined to tell me about his love affairs was probably not worth remembering. During the twilight of the Victorian era, his experience of *amour* might be considered remarkable; compared with the average experience of a healthy youth of the 1960s, my grandfather's record appears charmingly innocent. He knew many prostitutes and a few nice girls he could not sleep with; he knew his wife, as well as any man ever does, and he got to know several other women in stolen moments here and there later in his life. At no time, except with his wife, did he ever enjoy the kind of intimacy I shared with a half-dozen women before I was married. Sex out of wedlock was simply forbidden until the 1960s when we legitimized it per *force majeure,* by resacralizing erotic love. I was not in any way special. I would not use myself as an example here if my experience were not normal to the time.

Such an experience as ours may never be normal again.

No one can doubt the generation that came of age in the 1960s was graced with a privileged experience of Eros. If a certain shy schoolgirl of my acquaintance had been born thirty years earlier, she might well have become a nun; instead, the steamy climate forced her into an erotic blossom. If I had been born in the twenties, I probably would have married the first woman I slept with, à la Andy Hardy, and lived the rest of my days in a state of innocence more wide-eyed than my grandfather's. But as things turned out, many of us cultivated the belief our lovemaking was sacred, as sacred as anything to be found in church or synagogue, and we would have it with or without the blessing of rabbi or priest. The Song of Songs, which is Solomon's, was all the bible we needed, that song and the rocking tunes on the radio. This was revolutionary. We made love without fear or guilt.

If the history of an individual has meaning, the collective

experience of a generation must have profound historical consequences. It would be a sad thing if, to quote the tragic lines of T. S. Eliot, "We had the experience, but missed the meaning."

We have not missed the meaning of the sexual "revolution" or the "summer of love." That lascivious slow dance was to reawaken in us an awareness of human love and its bonding power, as well as love's generative nature, by beginning with the most obvious vibration, love's lowest common denominator—sex.

In every voluntary act of sexual love, there dwells a germ of the sacred. The orgasm is a moment of communication so intense as to dissolve the boundaries between two people; in this moment you attain a kind of liquid state unconscious of separate existence. The throbbing of the climactic moment greatly resembles the beating of a human heart, and the heart shapes of the organs of reproduction are meant to remind us of this: The climax of erotic excitement is the apotheosis of the mortal pulse.

But here is an important difference. You may listen to your heartbeat as if you stood outside it, as if the heartbeat were somehow detached. You cannot detach yourself from the pulse of an orgasm without a strained and unnatural effort, because you are *inside* the orgasm. There the mortal moment meets eternity. In that moment you dwell *within* the pulse of life, which is undeniably bigger than you are.

Experience this alone and you become aware of the truth of it for you. Experience this simultaneously with your beloved, and you may know the joy of fusing with another human being in a sacred zone of communication. Share this ecstasy with a succession of lovers during the period of a decade when most contemporaries are doing the same thing, making it acceptable, and you are part of an erotic revolution. During the 1960s this amounted to a transpersonal "meltdown" of ego boundaries. Outsiders who shriek that the promiscuity of the sixties was animalistic and profane have definitely missed the point. We are not a generation of Don Juans and Carmens, as you may see from our present demeanor. The erotic impulse cannot be satisfied with carnal pleasure; erotic love is designed for generation into the future.

We were on a spiritual quest which, like all spiritual journeys, must begin in the flesh. We were born into a world love seemed to have abandoned at the gates of Dachau and Auschwitz, and in the shadows of the atomic mushroom cloud. Eros had to shake, rattle, and roll us hard to get our attention, to remind us that the world would not end so long as we kept generating the future, physically and psychically.

I believe the veterans of the sexual revolution are, on the whole, better prepared for unselfish parenting and social altruism than any generation that has ever lived.

Though it was first proclaimed thousands of years ago, and I repeated the fact earlier in this chapter, permit me to rephrase this vital principle of the doctrine of love. Sexual desire can never be wholly satisfied with carnal pleasure, its first object. This colossal vibration of love is designed for regeneration in the future of the beloved, your own beloved, and all of humankind in the future.

Sex is essentially a sacred act.

four

CONJUGAL LOVE AND

ADULT FRIENDSHIP

When all is said and done, the best marriage is an adult friendship born and sustained in the spirit of Eros; and the best friendship is a marriage in every sense but the erotic.

At last we have come to a topic where the available doctrine can answer most of our questions. In a book full of mysteries, it should be a pleasure to find that friendship is not one of them. As Joseph Addison wrote in the eighteenth century, no subject of morality has been better handled than friendship. He had in mind the writings of Aristotle mostly, who got an idea or two from Pythagoras about friendship being an equality, and that friendship is like "one soul in two bodies."

The true friendship forms slowly, requiring close contact. But once it forms, the bond proves invulnerable to slander or mistrust. Only good people can aspire to great friendship, and the two candidates must be "equal"—that is, equal in virtue and independence.

Aristotle draws all of his characteristics of friendship from the way a good person relates to himself. The good man is truthful with himself, and so remains truthful with his friend. He is kind to himself, and becomes easygoing or demanding as life requires; and so he will be kind, generous, and inspiring to his friend. The good person may be as critical of his friend's actions as of his own. He will desire the well-being of his friend as he desires it for himself. Good friends have the same basic purposes in living, and will grieve and rejoice with one another. The good friend is, in truth, a second self.

Bad men and women cannot be friends. The bad man is at war with himself; we may go as far as to say the very soul of such a person is divided against itself. Wicked people cannot be real friends, because you cannot trust them. Today they violate the rights of a distant stranger, and tomorrow they doublecross you for their own profit. They lie to themselves in one breath, and then lie to you with the next. They promise to cover your back in a fight; you look around, and they have vanished, gone over to the enemy for a bribe.

The theory that good friends must be "equal" calls for some delicate explaining. Quite frankly, the idea makes many people uncomfortable, particularly in America where we are all supposed to be equal in every way.

Wealth, power, social position—these things often stand in the way of true friendship. I am fond of the African proverb "It is difficult to make friends with an elephant." The author was thinking of friendship with the king, but his words pertain to all relationships between unequals: the great one will step on the little one without even noticing. A man cannot really be friends with his boss, his servant, or his children; where a strict class system has survived, true friends usually come from the same social stratum. A frequent cause of a breakup between old friends is the worldly promotion of one of them, in wealth or honor. Envy endures as a powerful human motive, and few but the saints are entirely beyond reach of its barbs.

In the perfect friendship you can no more envy your friend than envy yourself.

Harmony of temperaments is a key to friendship, but there is little more we can say about it. People seem to be born with a certain capacity for happiness, which surfaces in adulthood, and you can often read it in a man or a woman's mature face. Cheerful people have an easier time getting along with each other than do melancholy couples. But misery loves company, and occasionally two miserable people will get along famously, grumbling a perfect duet. A person with a keen sense of humor can never bond perfectly with a friend who has none. Beyond these obvious sorts of generalization, the harmony of temperaments defies analysis for the simple reason that people sometimes seek in friends what they lack in themselves.

To give you some sense of the rarity of a pure friendship, philosophers claim that you cannot have more than one at any given time in your life. For what will you do if both cry out for help at once? And suppose one friend should tell you in confidence some news the other friend needs desperately to know?

In conclusion, let me call attention to the graceful word itself, the Anglo-Saxon word *friendship.* A state of characters, friendship is a vessel of two bodies, carrying their one soul to a single destination. It resembles a vessel moving through time. Insofar as love arises in friendship, love feels similar to the love a good person bears toward one's self or toward God. Unlike erotic love, the love between good friends remains a temperate fire, a constant flame that does not leap, flicker, or dwindle but is always gentle and smooth. Like the movement of a good ship on calm seas, it may be scarcely noticeable.

The goal of perfect friendship is to find out what is good and then do it, together.

MY BEST FRIEND

When I was in my junior year at college, in 1968, I returned to my dormitory room before dinner to find an envelope had been slipped under my door. I opened the envelope, and found inside a short poem.

Where I went to college, in that decade, poetry was far more popular than football. I wrote my share of verse, and was editor of the college literary magazine, so this was not at all unusual for me, to find student poems slipped under my door.

But this new work was remarkable in several ways. First of all, the poem was uncommonly well made; second, it was dedicated to me. The author had read something I had written, and evidently admired it. He had found a way of saying this in his little poem without being the least bit ironic or sentimental. He closed the communication with a straightforward invitation to friendship, and signed it with his name, David Lewis Bergman.

I was flattered and I was impressed. A face vaguely connected with the name, and the rumbling sound of a voice, came to mind. Ours was a small school, so it took me only five minutes to find the young poet in the dining hall.

David Lewis Bergman, freshman class of '72, was sitting by himself in front of a glass of milk. He looked as Pushkin must have looked as an old man, dark and hairy, with broad, almost African, Semitic features, black wide-set eyes with heavy brows that nearly touched above his great nose, and kinky hair on his head and his knuckles. He had the soft body of a powerful youth who by some quirk of development is prematurely out of condition at seventeen years of age. He did not look well or happy.

I told him I liked his poem, and he brightened a bit as he sipped the glass of milk. When he began to speak, after drawing asthmatic breaths in order to get up a good head of steam, he made a noise such as I never hope to hear again in my life—a rumbling, resonant basso profundo that seemed to come from nineteenth-century Russia by way of Oxford, England, and the upper east side of New York City.

This was the voice of someone resolutely determined to sound like no one who had ever spoken the King's English before him. In this, as in practically everything David Lewis Bergman would ever set his mind to, he was a glorious success and the talk of the whole college community. No one could figure out where the accent had come from; or, if it was an affectation, which it probably was, what this revealed about his character. Soon enough, people gave up on the mystery, because what Bergman had to say about literature, politics, economics, or horse-race handicapping was so fascinating you forgot how he sounded.

The milk was for his ulcer. Yes, he had an ulcer which he brought with him to the college. Bergman also had the gout and serious back trouble. I was richly impressed, and told him so. He might be one of those tormented geniuses like Keats, whose short life would force his art to flower early. He smiled and said he hoped not.

As we got up to walk out into the night air, talking together, he limped from his gout, bent over somewhat from his back trouble, and I had to resist the temptation to take him by the elbow, as if he were some distinguished octogenarian.

He probably will be a distinguished octogenarian when I am cold in the grave. For he got the worst part of old age over with when he was a teenager. How David Lewis Bergman grew from old age toward an eternal youthfulness is a story he will write some day himself; let it suffice here to say his childhood was a miserable one, being shadowed with ill health and family problems. But he had the presence of mind to invent a bright future for himself, and the courage to move into that life. These things I began to admire in him as our friendship slowly developed.

During my college years I was not very sociable. I was almost wholly dedicated to study, and the time I spent away from my books I passed in the company of Madeline Carter or Vivian Renka. I had a casual friend or two with whom I would have a cup of tea during quick study breaks. And I had buddies who would keelhaul me from the library to get me drunk at fraternity parties. But for me those college years were not a time for exploring intimate friendships with men. I had not yet figured myself out, and I knew that self-knowledge must be my first order of business.

David was doing the same thing, in his own way. But without being at all pushy, the younger man allowed me to know that the two of us were on the same ship. He began bringing me his poems on a regular basis, to hear what I had to say about them. They were very good poems and quickly got better. So when he offered to read and respond to my new work, I trusted his ears and eyes well enough to take him up on the offer.

Our friendship, in those early years, might best be described as a friendship of utility, a working association. It was not very personal. Our wide-ranging conversation never delved too deeply into the details of our backgrounds or the emotions that constitute personality. As I remember, the relation then was not even distinctly pleasurable, except that we flattered each other with our attention.

Working criticism is an abrasive process. At the most agreeable, it is like a day in which nothing memorable happens; at worst the activity is like having a tooth pulled without anesthetic. Without deep trust, such work is impossible; and without humor over a period of time the labor becomes unendurable. We have been at it now for a quarter of a century.

During the second year of our association, I had occasion to introduce David to my mother. She had come to visit me for a week in the little apartment I rented above a garage my last year of college.

These were small quarters, and when David showed up for work, there was no place for my mother to go. So after hasty introductions, she made herself comfortable on the couch, with a book and some knitting. And in the urgency of our business, David and I forgot all about her.

David was in a lather over something I had just written—*committed* is the word he would have used. It must have been rather long. The creation was just good enough to warrant his full attention, but so ungainly and ill favored, so full of rashes, diseases, and distempers, that only the most ingenious treatment might save it from extinction. David had arrived with the work mapped and annotated according to critical strategy. He was prepared to rescue my poem from me in all-out warfare, if it should come to that.

And so he began, his peculiar voice rumbling like a distant storm on the opposite end of the couch from where my mother sat, peaceably knitting. I listened, nodding, standing next to the stove. He started calmly enough, explaining how the poem had engaged his curiosity. But he quickly put aside these pleasantries, always the least important part of such a discussion. As he got on to the meat of his argument, Bergman warmed to the subject, and his volume increased. The walls shook. As he began to call attention to the poem's defects, his eyes flashed fire, and he began to thunder. He got to his feet orating, and shook his fist, now at me and then at the piece of paper, as if it had stuck its tongue out at him. "And this . . . and then *this*!" he roared, slapping the page, and gasping, moving toward me as I sidestepped him and circled to the other side of the stove. Then he would fall to laughing about the wondrous stupidity of some phrase or other, "Surely you don't mean *this* . . ." holding his sides until he could regain some composure, some resting place in which he could catch his asthmatic breath. From there he would regroup his forces to attack again, and so on, lecturing as I listened and nodded, holding up my hands now and then as you would to appease an advancing guard dog . . .

I had been through this routine enough times to understand

there was nothing personal about it. David was not really angry at me. It was the *language* that outraged him—this gorgeous, protean, demonic vocabulary and grammar of English that would not give us a moment's rest, that would always be hiding, fooling, and playing tricks on us, while here we were dedicating our lives to trying to make only a little bit of sense out of it, and maybe a thing of beauty. David was furious with the language, and with whatever god had drafted us into the service of such an impossible admiral, friends perforce on a leaky ship. If David had any feeling for me at all during these sessions, it was the same combination of admiration and pity he felt for himself. We were on the same ship, but God only knew where it was taking us.

When David had said all he had to say, I gave him a glass of milk which he drank rapidly. He exchanged a few polite words with my shell-shocked mother, and then excused himself for some other urgent business. He had to read a book or go and criticize someone else's poetry. I believe he had decided to read all twenty volumes of Browning by his twentieth birthday, and there are just so many hours in a man's day, what with sleeping a little and eating a little and correcting his friend's rude verses . . .

"Who was that awful boy?" my mother asked, raising her eyebrows. She was not accustomed to sitting quietly by, in a small room, while her only son was being attacked by a crazy Russian.

I did not really know what to tell her. Neither David nor I knew quite who we were in 1970, when I graduated from college and left him behind. But we had certainly helped each other to find out.

Before he graduated from college, David would give me a small book he had published, and on the title page he had scribbled an inscription that nearly defined us. It said we would work together to create a language of light and beauty. He was in fact destined for a distinguished literary and academic career. He entered the exclusive graduate program at the Johns Hopkins University, one of seven graduate fellows in English. Having fled my own graduate school, I arrived in Baltimore, on personal business, only a few months before my friend. Then it seemed the rarest of coincidences we found ourselves together again, five hundred miles away from that college in the Midwest.

I found David had grown slender, firm, and hearty. All of his features had sharpened. He had cultivated a youthful exuberance and joviality which now rarely deserts him. He now began to look as Pushkin must have looked as a young man, having at last found himself.

Since then, we have been constant companions. By the time we were in our early twenties, I knew myself well enough to be ready to know someone else, and our friendship of utility had prepared us well for graduate friendship. We discovered in due time we could confide in each other almost anything; and then we discovered that we could confide in each other absolutely everything, and this made both our lives easier. When I left for a year in Italy in 1976, he would take over all my correspondence—a job I would not entrust to anyone else in the world, if there were anyone else who would do it.

I can confide in David both the misfortunes that occur in my life, and the successes. This last is a true test of friendship, for I have found only a handful of people in my life who truly rejoice with me in triumph. Between David and me there can be no jealousy, for any triumph is always shared; the only successes that matter to us we have, in a real sense, achieved together, while striving for the same goals. This is essential to friendship in some degree, though friends' occupations need not be identical. I can never be intimate friends with a man or a woman who values money above wisdom or human life, or who lies for the sake of temporary convenience or personal profit. I cannot rejoice in their "success" because I do not believe in it. We are on different ships. David and I are on the same ship, and fair weather and favorable wind mean the same thing to both of us.

Often we are able to finish each other's sentences. We have continued our working relationship, editing each other's writing and advising each other in teaching, as we teach at the same university. But if by some misfortune he could no longer work, I would be no less devoted to him.

In manners and morals, I am surprised when I find myself on the opposite end of an ethical or a political argument with David. It makes me distrust myself, because we have always had similar ideals. People who care less about me, as well as those who fear me, will agree with my foolishness because they find it far easier not to dispute me—but not David. He performs one of the highest offices of friendship by serving as my second conscience, and I strive to do the same for him.

I so honor his values and judgment that he is my children's legal godfather and the executor of my will, for all it is worth, if I should die before him. And I hope that I do, as the world would seem a dreary place without his company.

MY WIFE

The most striking difference in the love I bear my wife, as contrasted with the love I feel for my friend, is that in the first there is so much of the physical.

I may miss my friend if we are apart for some time, but not anywhere near so much as I miss my wife, whose presence I feel viscerally. She quickens my pulse at times, and at other times I feel a tropical heat between us. My friend David and I love, if you will forgive a little poetry, as angels might who have no bodies—far different from my wife and I who contend, day in and day out, with the bittersweet burden of our flesh, which is a kind of maddening delight.

I fell in love with this woman on the same day I met her, a day that seemed most unlikely to end in the way it did.

I have already mentioned the peculiarity of the meeting. Madeline Carter, the first woman I ever fell in love with at first sight, introduced me to the second, her childhood friend Wendy Roberts, who became my wife and the mother of my children. Wendy and Madeline had been classmates at a private boarding school in Washington, D.C., lived in the same dormitory, and sang in that famous choir at the National Cathedral. They spent many of their vacations at Wendy's home on the Eastern Shore of Maryland. The love of music drew them together, and the life of the mind; by the time I met Madeline, the two women were friends of the sort that share the deepest secrets of the heart.

Wendy and I had heard a lot about each other, which I suppose always primes the pump for romance. She had gotten married very young, about the time I met Madeline, and the marriage had put a distance between the two women; Madeline always spoke of her old friend Wendy with a kind of wistfulness. She thought Wendy and I would like each other if we ever met, and the two of us would find many things in common, especially our childhood memories of the Eastern Shore of Maryland. Wendy had grown up there, a fact that intrigued me, with my mystical feelings about that part of the country.

She grew up not far from my grandparents' home on the Eastern Shore. But her marriage to a successful young novelist had put Wendy somewhat out of touch with her past, including the friends of her childhood. So it seemed unlikely I would ever meet her—though if the possibility ever presented itself, Madeline would be sure to get us all together.

Our chance came in the autumn of 1972.

Madeline had spent the summer in New Haven, where the friends enjoyed a reunion. Wendy's marriage had come apart.

Madeline and I had not been spending much time together, because I was still trying to work things out with Vivian. I had quit graduate school and moved to Baltimore, where I was glorying in my first total independence, and did not want to be defined by a relationship with anybody else. I was vague and evasive, not knowing my own mind or heart. Madeline was patient and exasperated with me by turns over the long-distance telephone, trying to get straight answers from me about my feelings when I had no answers to give her, while she assured me beyond any doubt she was getting on with her life.

Getting on with her life . . . Madeline wanted a family, she had plenty of men pursuing her, and she had career ambitions. She wanted me out of the picture if I was not intending to be squarely in it. This September, Madeline was going to Brasenose College in England to study philosophy. Her plane would be taking off from Friendship Airport in Baltimore; we wanted to see each other once more before she left. Wendy happened to be driving south to visit her mother in Easton, Maryland, so Madeline would ride along with her to Baltimore.

I did not get a chance to see Wendy Roberts when she dropped Madeline at my apartment in Baltimore. Wendy was on her way across the Bay Bridge to visit her mother—the plan was for all of us to meet at my mother's house in Washington the next day.

I remember little about the time I spent with Madeline before we went to my mother's house. Madeline had a terrible head cold, and was in poor spirits. I suppose that, however glad we may have been to see each other, this rendezvous must have seemed like a long goodbye. We had failed to make plans for the future together, and now she would be going across the ocean. Without any commitment, our future looked hopeless, a dead end. Under the circumstances, I am sure each of us must have been making every effort to console and encourage the other during that long night and as we set out the next day from Baltimore to my mother's house in Washington.

Wendy met us there in the late afternoon. She knocked on the front door, and as my mother went to let her in, Wendy put her face to the picture window of the living room, cupped her hands against the glare, and looked in at us. I distinctly remember my impression that she looked like a happy pumpkin, with her round face.

When she came in the door to shake my mother's hand and then mine, I could see that roundness was something of a motif in her general appearance, though she was extremely small at the waist. Wendy was wearing jeans and turtleneck, a uniform of the period, and a leather cap with a buttoning visor, which was unbuttoned; as she took off the hat, an abundance of chestnut-colored, shining curls burst from under it, wildly framing the round cheeks and the high, broad forehead. Her eyes were very wide-set, blue-gray, and soft, and the rest of her coloring was unforgettably beautiful, vivid lips and cheeks against pale skin.

She looked like a Florentine painting of a cherub, somewhat androgynous at first, in the leather newsboy's cap, the jeans, and black turtleneck. This was an early 1970s unisex look, altogether unconvincing on Wendy's voluptuous figure. Also, she gave the impression of being younger than she was. She would always give that impression—having something to do with the roundness, the generosity of the lips and plump cheeks that one associates with children . . .

So I was stunned by the sound of her voice. I thought it was ventriloquism or my ears were deceiving me. The voice would have served a young man very well, being low and resonant enough, or a large woman in her forties steeped in brandy and cigarette smoke.

I find it hard now to remember exactly what I noticed, and when, or how I behaved. I know that everyone had lots to say, especially the three women, Madeline and Wendy being old friends, and my mother and Wendy having grown up just a few miles from each other's homes on the Eastern Shore. I must have been glassy-eyed in admiration of Madeline's friend who, in removing her sweater and taking a turn or two around the living room, commenting with polite interest on the pictures and bric-a-brac, revealed herself as one of the most perfectly *formed* human beings I had ever seen in my life. She gave new meaning to the Latin word for beauty, which is *forma*. Every part of her body—arms, legs, feet and hands, and particularly the roundness of her feminine characteristics—looked as if it had been labored over by a sculptor charged with defining the body's perfection forever. She was aware of this, which may have prompted the unisex disguise; anything less neutral would be downright provocative. Later that evening she would dress more revealingly, and the effect upon total strangers in a barroom would be a little frightening.

I suppose I was polite enough. But now I remember a good deal of my energy in that first hour must have gone toward mounting a defense against the invasion. I believe I must have been a little angry at this young woman, who packed more sexual energy per square inch of flesh than most attractive women contain in their whole mass. I already had a lot on my mind, and I did not need any more trouble. I kept trying not to look at her.

My mother is resourceful in such predicaments, and managed to get us down on the floor looking at old photographs, while we listened to the Beatles on the record player. This gave me something to do to take my mind off my difficulties, something to look at besides Wendy Roberts, though it was not all that much help. Even when I was not looking right at her, her sexual presence was about as subtle as the heat of a coal furnace.

While my mother put the finishing touches on the dinner of pot roast and potatoes, I identified the faces in the old snapshots, as Madeline and Wendy pointed to them in humor and wonder. The two women were marvelous together, laughing and teasing, no more concerned with my inner turmoil than if I had been a foreign guide through some fascinating and exotic museum. There was my father, toothless, under a crash helmet in a racing car . . . There was my mother, outside the Playland Amusement Arcade . . .

And by the time we sat down to dinner, I had begun to feel almost comfortable with the beautiful stranger.

THE BEAUTIFUL STRANGER

After dinner we said goodbye to my mother and drove to Baltimore to spend the eve of Madeline's departure together in my tiny apartment.

As we mounted the stairs to my door on the third floor of the brownstone building, I can tell you that the situation was, to put it mildly, highly charged with promises and threats not easy to imagine today. Remember this was twenty years ago, when it was not uncommon for healthy young people of various sexes to end up in the same bed at the drop of a hat, or a blouse or a pair of trousers—and think no less of one another the next morning. These were women of the highest character and morals. But there was only a single bed in the small room I welcomed them to in the twilight, a space that, to me, fairly shouted erotic possibilities.

My recent difficulties with Madeline did not help to clarify our roles. Wendy must have known as much about this as her friend could tell her—that Madeline and I were still lovers if no longer in love—because the two women were intimate as sisters. Yet by the time we reached my apartment, I suspected the sexual vibrations I was getting from the beautiful stranger whose roundness I followed up the stairs did not result solely from my admiration of *her*. I hurried to put a record on the stereo, Bessie Smith singing "Frosty Morning Blues," but the record did not help. Buttoning on a blouse of sheer Indian gauze, Wendy smiled at me over her shoulder. There was a full circuit. I realized I had done something to arouse Wendy, and she was sending as much voltage as she was receiving. But she would not, under any circumstances, encroach uninvited upon her friend's erotic territory. If invited, her smile seemed to say, that would be another story altogether.

As for Madeline, I think, looking back on it from a distance of twenty years, she had already given up on me. "Enough of this bozo," she might have told her friend, either in so many words or with a nod and a glance. "He's wasted enough of my time. Now let him waste yours if you like . . ."

I suggested the bar around the corner, O'Henry's, a neighborhood saloon across from the music conservatory. This was a homey, eccentric dive with sawdust and peanut shells on the floor and Rod Stewart wailing on the juke box, a hangout where the conservatory students mingled with the street characters, gypsies, cops, and hustlers. And you could dance, or play chess in a corner, or get into the most bizarre conversations.

On the way I noticed my lovely companions were dressed in very different roles and moods. Madeline, in a long, loose shift of cotton print, in flat shoes, looked modest, almost prim, an attractive librarian out on the town. Wendy, in a sheer blouse and short leather skirt, jacked up on heels, stepping into O'Henry's saloon, was a moving target for the eyes of every male who ever lusted for a woman of legal age. As Madeline and I followed her through the smoky room, I watched as men spun on their barstools to get an eyeful of Wendy. I have never seen anything like it. I thought I was going to have to kill somebody before I could get the woman home.

But this was a civilized bar, jumping with music students and tame drunks. I ordered beer, and we toasted one another—Madeline, Wendy, and I—and we called for more beer, and drank, et cetera.

And when they had finished off a pitcher or so of beer, they wanted to dance to the music on the juke box. Wendy put quarters into the machine. I danced with Madeline while Wendy watched. Then I danced with Wendy.

I suppose we began decently enough, moving together to the slow music. But our fingers entwined, my hand on the small of Wendy's perfect back, her round cheek against mine felt such intense heat that the two of us seemed to melt quickly. Dizziness made us cling to each other more tightly so we would not fall down. I have described the liquid state achieved by two people in the act of making love, the ego meltdown—for some couples this is meant to happen in the instant of their first embrace, and Wendy and I are one of those couples. Her eyelids drooped, as did mine; and as we danced, her body molded itself to mine, hills to hollows, as if the two of us were soft clay. Dancing, we seemed to be making love, and there could be no question that the one would lead quickly to the other.

After more beer and more dancing, we made our way home, the three of us arm in arm. I put a record on the machine and we danced some more, sometimes all of us together, and drank the beer in the refrigerator. Madeline went out on the fire escape to look at the stars, while Wendy and I danced and whispered about the amazement of merely touching. We ran down the stairs of the old apartment building so I could show her the fountain in the park across the street. We sat by the fountain at one o'clock in the morning, and we kissed for the first time, a kiss so soul searching and intoxicating that neither of us has ever quite been able to finish it.

We returned to the little apartment, hand in hand, and were somewhat embarrassed to find Madeline asleep on the top mattress she had placed on the floor.

Wendy and I undressed each other, with electric fingers, and lay down on the boxspring staring at each other, and up into the darkness, our bodies on fire. We embraced and our fingers explored each other, but we did not venture further. We must be alone for that; and however magnanimous her friend had been, it would be a rank violation to make love to me in the same room with Madeline, when Wendy and I had been introduced only hours before. So much for the morality of the period.

Next morning our hangovers left us little energy for conversation. There were hugs and kisses, and goodbyes, some tentative and some final. Wendy and I found enough privacy to make plans to finish what we had started. After driving Madeline to the airport, Wendy had to return to Connecticut. But she would be back to see me the next weekend.

Wendy was working at a jewelry store in New Haven, and her boss let her out early on Friday afternoon so she could drive nonstop to Baltimore. Arriving near midnight, she knocked on my door.

I opened my door to find Wendy, grinning from ear to ear, though exhausted, and her dog, who was even more exhausted, panting. The poor black labrador was obviously pregnant and ready to drop its litter any day. At that moment I had mixed feelings about this young woman, for all her beauty, this woman in a man's flannel shirt, hair like a mop, and her dog who circled the room looking for a place to nest.

I had not seen the bewitching creature in a week, and the events of the previous weekend had begun to develop a patina of disturbing unreality.

I let the dog go down the fire escape, and when she returned Wendy made a bed for her in a corner of the kitchen.

She said the trip had been a long one, with her poor dog, who had to be let out every few miles upon the urgency that vexes every pregnant lady. Wendy was tired and hungry after the long, long drive.

I told her I would do everything I could do to make it worth her while.

Leaving the dog, we went out and walked through the park past the fountain where we had kissed the weekend before. Nearby was an all-night diner where we ordered hamburgers, and talked, nervously, with the shyness of two people for whom Eros has arranged an adventure and destiny without their consent, two people for whom talking seems almost dishonest, an evasion or postponement of a necessary action. We ate quickly, looking into each other's eyes, and took long strides in returning to my apartment. No sooner had we closed the door than we were out of our clothes and in each other's arms.

What we did, and how we did it, I will not attempt to describe because that would take me far from my purpose. As I have said elsewhere, this is not that kind of book. But I must try to tell you what distinguishes this experience from every other sexual encounter in my life, and how I knew it was *more* than erotic, triggering an emotion I would soon recognize as conjugal love. As I entered the body of this beautiful stranger for the first time, I had two sensations—one purely physical and the other visionary—and I can remember the experience in that narrow bed as if it had happened an hour ago. First, the sheer physical pleasure of this young woman's flesh holding mine was so much more intense than I had ever known, it seemed I had never made love before, that all other sex had been mere shadow play. Second, I had a clear inner vision of movement: I was falling into a bottomless cavern, now and then grasping an overhanging branch which would halt my descent briefly, until the branch giving way would leave me falling again, deeper, deeper . . .

We hardly slept at all that night, or the next. Falling led to climbing, as each climax delivered us to a higher landing where we would rest briefly before desire would set us climbing again. We could not get enough of the taste of each other's flesh, and as we made love, we got better at arousing each other. For twenty-four hours we did not leave the bed, as dawn came and the sun found us making love, throwing wild shadows upon the furniture, the carpet, the walls, and the sun left us making love in the twilight. Just before midnight of the second day of feasting on each other, we realized, hilariously, that we were both starving. Hollow-eyed, tousle-haired, throwing on the legal minimum of clothing, we hurried to the bar to gobble down a sandwich, quickly to stoke the fires, so we would have the strength to return to bed and make love again. You have seen this young couple before somewhere, and you would be more or less than human if you did not envy them.

No one could ever be more happy than we were during those nights and days of discovery. I found that Wendy was not only beautiful but wise and good—I guess I had expected all of this from Madeline's close friend. In the intervals between lovemaking, Wendy talked, in her low melodious voice, of her childhood on the Eastern Shore, the sights and sounds of the tidal marshes I knew from my own childhood. She told of her grandparents' gracious estate, and how she and her sisters had gone with their mother to live there after her father's tragic death when Wendy was four years old. And she talked of her marriage at the age of nineteen, and how it had broken up a year later. She told me of her ambitions, to go to art school, to become a painter; how her mother had been an artist; and her grandfather had designed the lighting fixtures in famous buildings, Radio City Music Hall . . . She spoke with clarity and wonderful humor, until I would stop her words with kisses.

When the time came for her to leave on Sunday, all we could think was how and when we could be together again.

Actually I had a lot of other things on my mind. I was twenty-two years of age, and free, and had every intention of remaining a bachelor. Now I felt I had been run over by a truck, erotically speaking. This Wendy Roberts was simply too beautiful and thrilling to be believed, and so I began organizing my defenses to disbelieve her. I would revive old relationships with attractive women to create interference. I would call my friend David Bergman on the phone, and tell him I had been bewitched by Venus herself, and try to get him to talk me out of my madness (which he would not do once he had met her). I would do anything I could do to save myself before I careered altogether out of control and into a domestic situation from which nothing could extricate me.

But I was already in that situation, after one weekend with my future wife, as we kissed each other goodbye on that October afternoon. As coolly and calmly as we could, Wendy and I decided we would decide nothing, and get together again whenever it was convenient . . .

Two weeks later Wendy's mother was in a car accident and broke her jaw, and Wendy had to leave New Haven for Maryland, so she could nurse her mother back to health.

Now she was only seventy miles away, across the Bay Bridge. I was magnetically drawn to her, and she would hardly let me leave. In Wendy's childhood bedroom under the eaves of her mother's house, we continued our lovemaking throughout the autumn, as the moon shone clear on us through the dormer windows that overlooked a tidal river. Lying on the tiny bed, she would press her naked feet against the sloped ceiling as I floated above her and I thought the room would explode. We made love as if we would turn our bodies into a single sweet substance, liquid or solid, or as if separation were an unendurable agony.

After her mother got well, Wendy moved to Baltimore, to an apartment four blocks from mine. We fixed meals together, ate together, slept now at her apartment and then at mine—insofar as we slept. In the mornings we parted for work, to meet again at twilight. We became not only lovers but friends, sharing housework, worries, and triumphs.

After several years of this, and a few brief separations that suited neither of us, we decided to move in together and dispense with the birth control. It was messy and unhealthy and just too much of a bother. While marriage seemed beside the point, a child appeared to us like the logical result, the inevitable outcome of all this lovemaking, the only perfect expression of its meaning.

And no sooner had we given up on the birth control than we got pregnant, which somehow surprised us.

The day we found out Wendy was pregnant began in celebration and ended in argument. I just assumed that we would get married, and wanted to shout it from the rooftops. But Wendy assumed nothing of the kind.

WHY WE ARGUED ABOUT MARRIAGE

The institution of marriage is full of inhospitable ghosts. I was more or less willing to live with them, and Wendy was dead set against it. I sure picked the right person to argue with.

A young modern couple who have been living together for a year and a half, may know the perfect bliss of conjugal affection until the day they decide to get married. That day they are sure to run into certain emotional difficulties, if they are as reflective and independent as we were in 1976.

Why?

Because they are only twenty-five years of age, and the marriage they are about to enter, and hope to live in for the next few decades, is probably one hundred times older than they are.

Not only is the *institution* ancient, but the young couple's knowledge of marriage comes primarily from their parents, who are twice as old as the lovers. Old, old, old. The day the young couple decides to get married, they look at their parents' marriages, and their grandparents', and they look at the grim words of the ceremony, "in sickness and in health . . . till death do us part . . ." And suddenly, these darling young people get butterflies in their stomachs, and wonder aloud whether marriage is really such a good idea after all.

No wonder so many of us in the sixties got married in an open meadow, with no witnesses more important than the trees and flowers. Marriage is a fine old idea. But marriage has seen some hard times, and conjugal love has barely survived through the last fifteen hundred years of institutional weddings without losing the instinctive fire and zeal it must have known in prehistory.

Let history speak for itself.

Then the Lord God said, *It is not good that the man should be alone; I will make him an help meet for him.*

—GENESIS 2:18

For the man is not of the woman; but the woman of the man.
Neither was the man created for the woman; but the woman for the man.

—I CORINTHIANS 11:8–9

I will greatly multiply thy sorrow and thy conception; in sorrow thou shalt bring forth children; and thy desire shall be to thy husband, and he shall rule over thee.

—GENESIS 3:16

Who can find a virtuous woman? for her price is far above rubies.
The heart of her husband doth safely trust in her, so that he shall have no need of spoil.

—PROVERBS 31:10–11

Wives, submit yourselves unto your own husbands, as unto the Lord.
For the husband is head of the wife, even as Christ is the head of the church: and he is the saviour of the body.
Therefore as the church is subject unto Christ, so let the wives be to their own husbands in every thing.
Husbands, love your wives, even as Christ also loved the church, and gave himself for it.

—EPHESIANS 5:22–25

I say therefore to the unmarried and widows, It is good for them if they abide even as I.
But if they cannot contain, let them marry: for it is better to marry than to burn.

—I CORINTHIANS 7:8–9

Man hath three joys—praise, wisdom and glory: which three things are overthrown and ruined by woman's art. . . . Woman was evil from the beginnings, a gate of death, a disciple of the servant, the devil's accomplice, a fount of deception, a dogstar of godly labors, rust corrupting the saints; whose perilous face hath overthrown such as had already become almost angels.

—Salimbene, a Franciscan (1221–88)

The character of men is stronger than that of women and can bear the attacks of enemies better, can stand strain longer, is more constant under stress. . . . Women, on the other hand, are almost all timid by nature, soft, slow, and therefore more useful when they sit still and

147

watch over our things. It is as though nature thus provided for our well-being, arranging for men to bring things home and for women to guard them. The woman as she remains locked up at home, should watch over things by staying at her post, by diligent care and watchfulness. The man should guard the woman, the house and his family and country, but not by sitting still. He should exercise his spirit and his hands in brave enterprise, even at the cost of sweat and blood.

—Leon Battista Alberti, *The Family In Renaissance Florence*
(15th Century)

When I look beside myself I see my brothers and sisters and friends, and I find that there's nothing but godliness in marriage. The longing of man for a woman is God's creation—that is to say, when nature's sound, not when it's corrupted as it is among Italians and Turks.

—Martin Luther (16th Century)

Female government has never done any good. God made Adam master over all creatures, to rule over all living things, but when Eve persuaded him that he was lord even over God she spoiled everything. We have you women to thank for that! With tricks and cunning women deceive men, as I, too, have experienced.

—Martin Luther (16th Century)

I am rich, God has given me my nun [his wife] and three children; what care I if I am in debt, Katie [his wife] pays the bills. . . . George Kark has taken a rich wife and sold his freedom. I am luckier, for when Katie gets saucy, she gets nothing but a box on the ear.

—Martin Luther (16th Century)

ANTRONIUS: It's not feminine to be brainy.
MAGDALIA: Isn't it a wife's business to manage the household and rear the children?
ANTRONIUS: It is.
MAGDALIA: Do you think she can manage so big a job without wisdom?
ANTRONIUS: I suppose not.
MAGDALIA: But books teach me this wisdom. . . .

ANTRONIUS: I've often heard the common saying, "A wise woman is twice foolish."

MAGDALIA: That's commonly said, yes, but by fools.

—Erasmus, *Council of Women, Colloquies*

A bride must be made to realize that on leaving the tutelage of her family she passes under that of her husband.

—Napoleon Bonaparte

The husband must possess the absolute power and right to say to his wife: "Madam, you shall not go out, you shall not go to the theatre, you shall not receive such and such a person; for the children you will bear shall be mine."

—Napoleon Bonaparte

This principle was applied to the [Napoleonic] code to the fullest degree: wives were subject to their husbands, had no rights in the administration of common property, were forbidden to give, sell, or mortgage property, and could acquire property only with their husbands' written consent. Napoleon imposed on French society his view that women must be treated as irresponsible minors throughout their lives.

—J. Christopher Herold, *The Age of Napoleon*

Women should stick to knitting.

—Napoleon Bonaparte

She who has been used to pent bounds of her desires as a general principle, will have learned to withstand a passion for dress and personal ornaments; and the woman who has conquered this propensity has surmounted one of the most domineering temptations which assail the sex. Modesty, simplicity, humility, economy, prudence, liberality, charity, are almost inseparable, and not very remotely connected with an habitual victory over personal vanity.

—Hannah More, 1792

In the educated woman the nervous system has been developed at the expense of other bodily organs and structure. The delicate organism and sensitive and highly developed nervous system of our girls was

never intended by the creator to undergo the stress and strain of the modern system of higher education, and the baneful results are becoming more and more apparent as the years go by.
—Ralph W. Parsons, "The American Girls Versus Higher Education,
Considered From A Medical Point Of View,"
New York Medical Journal (1907)

The full force of sexual desire is seldom known to a virtuous woman.
—William Sanger, *A History of Prostitution*

Patriarchy, polygamy, marriage without love, spiritual love without sex—these are the ghosts that still haunt the modern altar of matrimony.

And these are some of the reasons my wife and I argued about marriage. In addition to the historical arguments, there was Wendy's more recent history, a failed marriage which had soured her on the subject of marriage in general. But Wendy was particularly sensitive to the difficulties our child might encounter with society if we did not marry, a difficulty no one can deny. Pressing this point, I did not so much win the argument as succeed in wearing her down, showing Wendy that her aversion to marriage was not nearly so great as my desire for it.

So we got on the phone and told everyone our plans.

LOVERS AND FRIENDS

From the night I met Wendy until several years after we had been married, the two of us were fairly besotted, blinded with erotic passion for each other.

I would not have had it any other way. But Eros did sometimes foil our desire to become friends. Those were years of intense excitement, a roller-coaster ride of joy and confusion as we struggled to become friends of the sort I described in the first two pages of this chapter—one soul in two bodies.

Marriage presents a unique challenge to the partners, which I will consider as a paradox; if we can resolve the paradox, then we may discover a doctrine of conjugal love.

Lovers swept together and into the future by erotic passion, remain under the domination of Eros, excepting those brief interludes of afterglow, when their desire has been slaked and they rest awaiting the next tremors of lust. Erotic love begins in the desire for possession, and ends in possession, the moment the lover becomes one with the object he or she desires. Happily the impulse rises again out of its ashes, like the phoenix; for Eros, as we have seen, strives for the permanent, recurrent possession of the beautiful—momentary possession does not satisfy the powerful spirit.

Nevertheless, the primary impulse of erotic love is *to possess*: I never wanted anything so much as I wanted the beautiful stranger Wendy Roberts. I will even say I wanted her all the more *because* she was a beautiful stranger. Insofar as she inspires me twenty years later with lust, I can explain that she remains separate, strange, a thing to be possessed if only for an instant.

Now you can see how far this passion, with all its potential for explosive violence, stands afield from the steady fires of the perfect friendship. I never for a moment desired to possess my friend David Bergman. The notion seems absurd, because from the time I came to understand his character he became, to me, a second self with congruent values, ideas, and goals. Though we never experience the brief ecstasy of carnal union, in an important way we can never be separated. I am true to him so long as I remain true to myself; and insofar as I maintain a virtuous self-possession, I possess the only part of him that ever mattered to me—his mind and spirit.

But Wendy and I would struggle, and we have struggled, with the sweet burden of our flesh. Sex can be a delusion. Having possessed your partner for a moment of paradise in the marriage bed, you rise, pull on your shirt and trousers, and move in the direction of friendship. Yet you remain under the domination of Eros; you are in a mode of possession. The beautiful stranger at your side, so recently yours, is yours no longer. She belongs to herself, body and spirit, and must move into a space where you cannot follow her and do not belong. Maybe now is the time for her to bake the bread or nurse the baby. Maybe it is time for her to go to her studio and make a painting or a poem that has nothing to do with you. Or maybe she must hurry to the bed of another lover, for her life and desires are far more complicated and rich than you could understand because the two of you are not yet one soul in two bodies, perfect friends of the quality we described earlier.

Jealousy is a keen enemy of conjugal love; and sexual jealousy, a gross shape of it. Lovers moving from desire for possession to a moment of union, then back again to their natural separateness, may suffer pain and sadness after the bliss of union—for a moment they felt they were one in body and spirit. Now leaving the bedroom, the lovers are frustrated their union was temporary. Still in the mode of possession, husband or wife may covet what they may possess only in that instant of carnal union—the physical destiny and presence of the beloved. This is the madness of jealousy, wanting the body of another person for longer than the instant of an embrace. Having one body is enough trouble for any mortal, without being tormented over someone else's. The same jealousy that makes a woman despise her husband's secretary, makes the man dread his wife's success in the boardroom.

How do marriage partners, joined in erotic passion, ever cultivate true friendship? Must they give up the one relation in order to have the other? Surely lovers cannot become friends until they can see each other clearly, because friendship is a state of character, two characters: you cannot be friends with someone whose character you fail to see because lust has blinded you. Perhaps this is why so many good marriages begin in friendship *before* falling under the befuddling influence of Eros. In all honesty, it took Wendy and me several years to see each other clearly because we remained drunk on each other's flesh.

In our case, hard work became the solvent of our erotic obsession. The world of 1976 presented a number of challenges to the young lovers, poor and pregnant. As much as we might have liked, we could not spend our lives in bed. We had to get out into the daylight and work, sometimes separately and sometimes together, finding an apartment for a couple with a baby, painting a room, writing a book to pay the landlord and the grocer, making the dinner and washing the dishes.

Working by myself forced me to concentrate upon a worthy interest that was not my wife; working together with her, side by side, led us to concentrate on goals, physical and spiritual, outside of ourselves: making a living, raising children—goals in respect to which we must regard each other in a new light. I began to see clearly what I might always have suspected: that, aside from her intoxicating beauty, my wife was a human being with values, dreams, and ideas similar to my own. Hard work introduces young lovers to each other, delivering them from the erotic mode of possession, unsuitable to work, to the more spiritual practice of friendship. They must be friends, in order that they may work together.

Yet Eros is a colossal spirit, not easily put to flight. By day it teases the young couple as they try to work, making them blush. And by night when the work is put aside and the food and wine have restored their ardor, Eros leads the lovers by candlelight or moonlight back to bed again, into that frenzied mode of possession, now all the more intense after hours of separation.

The paradox of conjugal love is that lovers should become friends, and that friends should remain lovers. Erotic love being a mode of possession, and possession being at war with the principles of pure friendship, conjugal love would appear to be a logical impossibility.

Yet conjugal love is not only a possibility, it is a fact witnessed by millions of fortunate couples who are friends by day and lovers by night. For the true marriage proceeds upon two vectors, the physical and the spiritual. Erotic love enables us to transcend our physical strangeness, and friendship provides a resolution of spiritual separation. Conjugal love, unlike pure friendship, is not monolithic: it is dual, a spiritual tree firmly rooted in the flesh of this world, linking us both above and below.

As such, this emotion is often the greatest single factor in the education of the individual psyche from sexual maturity until the hour of death.

INTIMACY AND PRIVACY

When I was growing up, my mother never knew where my father was unless he was in the same room with her.

She learned, after they had been married for a while, not to ask him where he had been, where he was going, or what time she might expect him. It was none of her business. My father's business required the utmost discretion. So, for that matter, did his safety and hers. He was prepared for a number of situations in which she might thank God she did not know where he was or what he was doing; thus, she might look a stranger in the eye and say she had no knowledge of her husband's whereabouts.

My father would tell my mother what she needed to know. And while these breadcrumbs of information hardly satisfied her hunger to know what her husband did all day and half the night, I guess what he told her must have served their conjugal purposes, just as long as my father knew where *she* was, and knew my mother would be there waiting for him when he got home.

So in this, as in so many other details, my parents' marriage illustrates a prehistoric paradigm that is now passé, though its cause may persist. My father was obsessive about his privacy. And though his profession justifies the obsession somewhat, I think he would have been just as secretive if he had been an airplane pilot or a tax lawyer. My mother is politely discreet, and her ego is sharply drawn enough that she takes pleasure in her own privacy, the excitement of secrets she will take with her to the grave. But she had grown up in a house with parents who enjoyed the healthy intimacy of lovers who were good friends; she must have been terribly disappointed when my father shut her out of so much of his life and thought. Disappointed, when she had gotten over her astonishment.

My mother has told me that one of her earliest and most pleasant memories of her own parents is of their after-hours conversations under the sheets. Through the bedroom wall she could hear them whispering, talking, giggling until late into the night, and she tells me the sound was sweeter music to her ears than any lullabye.

All I heard my parents do at night was quarrel.

And I heard the same quarrel over and over and over, maddening in its simple monotony. My mother, after being home all day with no one to talk to but children, wanted to talk to my father. She wanted him to talk to her. And he would neither listen, nor would he talk to my mother, until he learned to talk, which did not happen until I was grown and the marriage was already in tatters.

From everything I have heard and read, in a thousand conversations and a hundred books on marriage by authorities on the subject, this same quarrel goes on nightly in nine tenths of the troubled marriages around the world. The wife wants desperately to talk to her husband—about the children, the budget, the dog, the refrigerator, love, death, about *anything* for God's sake—and all the husband wants to do is make love, or go to sleep, or watch the ball game, or stare at the goldfish.

He turns off his hearing aid.

"Why won't he *talk* to me, doctor? Why won't he *listen*? Is there something wrong with me?"

Nothing is wrong with the woman who wants to talk to her husband, or with the husband who wants silence. They are like most other couples in the world. But if the man does not begin to talk to her a little, and she does not begin to honor his privacy, they cannot generate the conjugal affection they need to make the marriage work.

There are marriages in which these roles are reversed, in which the man wants to communicate while the woman "dummies up." I have heard rumors of such marriages, though I cannot say I have ever seen one at first hand, and I rather suspect the rumors of their existence are exaggerated.

My wise uncle, married to my equally wise aunt, was just as obsessive about his privacy as my father. You would think my uncle had less reason. My uncle was a war hero of the rare sort that makes the word *hero* sound tinny, unfit for the reality. He was one of the few paratroopers who returned home from France after the Battle of the Bulge, which he survived at twenty years of age, carrying home with him a load of shrapnel in his leg. He went to the university on the G.I. Bill; and after several years of teaching and public school administration, my uncle became the dean of a college on the Eastern Shore. He settled there in a small town with my wise aunt, and they raised three fine children in model respectability.

You would think the man had nothing to hide. Theirs was the finest young marriage of which I had intimate knowledge in my boyhood, despite my uncle's oracular capacity for silence. He is the most articulate, sensitive, and compassionate educator and paratrooper who ever survived the Battle of the Bulge in France. But without warrant my uncle would go for days and sometimes weeks without speaking to my aunt, while she would have opened a vein and given a quart of blood for a few sentences from him.

I do not know whether my aunt ever considered leaving my uncle. If she did, I never heard anything about it. She hated the silence but loved my uncle so deeply she learned to live with it like a poor relation, an elderly in-law whom she knew must die eventually and leave the married couple again in a blissful intimacy. I think my aunt must have understood what my uncle, as a young paratrooper, could not have told her: the silence that seemed to separate them was not so much a barrier as a *part of the man*. This was a private conversation my uncle was having with himself upon which she must not intrude until it was finished. The young veteran had a great deal to discuss with himself after the Battle of the Bulge, not the least of which was the problem of evil, and the question of living or dying when he had been forced to deal with so many who had died. And then living, in 1948, may have seemed like an unfair accident. What exactly was he living for?

These were not topics he would discuss with his wife when they were young, any more than he could ventilate his inexorable confusions about erotic love. My wise uncle and aunt had been childhood sweethearts who plighted their troth before he went away to war. And she had waited for him to come home. If my uncle was not in some turmoil over the paradoxes of erotic love, as a twenty-year-old veteran of the war in Europe, he was surely the *only* man in my extended family for three generations who was not. The fact is that on both sides of my family every man has chafed at the bit of monogamy, and now and then one has slipped his traces, though we are not in the business of divorce.

Had I been that young veteran of the war in Europe, who

at twenty-five years of age looked like John Wayne in his prime, I might well have suffered some dark and deliciously overwhelming erotic confusions before I attained my conjugal wisdom and found myself gratefully "beyond all that." Whether my uncle arrived at his Buddhahood of monogamous wisdom by the road of carnal adventure or meditation matters little. He will never tell me, and I will never ask him. Yet I believe some of his privacy, and the silence that so tormented my patient aunt, can be explained only by his occult study of Eros.

My father's infidelities were notorious. My mother knew nothing of his other women until a decade of marriage had gone by. And the knowledge hurt her feelings for the few years she needed to realize that his love for other women had nothing whatever to do with her. Then my father's love for other women became just one more thing he did when he was not home, like brushing his teeth or reading a book. By an accident of congenial temperaments, the woman my father most loved in the world besides my mother became my mother's dear friend; and when the mistress was dying, my mother spent more time at the woman's bedside than did my father, who was typically preoccupied with making money for all of these women and children.

My handsome grandfather was remarkably open with me in discussing the many delights and confusions of Eros. He continued to be tempted by women of all ages until he was well into his seventies. And then the old gentleman revealed to me, with some sadness, that his efforts to resist this one, and that one, were not always so successful as his devotion to my grandmother deserved. He regretted this frailty in himself, and it is one of the few regrets I know he carried with him to his grave.

Many men get married before they have learned the lessons of Eros necessary to rest easily in the erotic lap of conjugal love.

I believe the monogamous condition of conjugal love, when it rests comfortably upon the married lovers, is a state of spiritual evolution all of us must envy if we have yet to attain it.

I was determined to be a better husband than my father had been.

In all fairness to my late father, he was an excellent father to me but a terrible husband to my mother. Not the worst, but certainly no husband for anyone to choose as a role model. For role models I had my wise uncle, though he was a little too taciturn; and I had my very handsome and gentle grandfather, whose only drawback as a role model is that he was a bit more subservient to my strong grandmother than suited my tastes.

As a husband, I designed to be kind and accessible like my grandfather. I would do my share of housework. I would *communicate* with my partner in life. For, after all, is this not the primary reason for marriage—to communicate with another human being, to share joys and sorrows? Is this not the goal of marriage—to achieve the intimacy that would draw me out of my shell, dissolve the ego barrier that not only protected me but made me a prisoner of my flesh?

I certainly married the right person. Wendy grew up in a home where sharing was so natural as to go unnoticed. Unlike the household of my boyhood, Wendy's home in the green countryside had been relatively free of strife.

After her father's death, Wendy's mother, the young widow Roberts, came to raise her three daughters in a charming cottage on her ancestral estate. There were difficulties, to be sure, for the widow dependent upon a tyrannical mother and frugal father, in the rarefied society of Talbot County, Maryland, in the 1950s. But these seemed only to draw the family closer together. The widow did not remarry so she had no husband to disagree with her. She created a household of cheerful, generous women who lived in civilized isolation in a modest abundance of love and annuities.

No one's door there was ever closed. Everyone's food and clothing and even most of their thoughts belonged to all. They respected privacy, when demanded; but secrecy to them was wickedness, pure and simple, almost on the same level as selfishness and certainly cut from the same cloth. Selfishness was nearly unthinkable in a loving family where it was "one for all and all for one." Theirs was not a house in which you would overhear an argument about who ate the last lamb chop.

So Wendy, in the first years of our courtship, was in for some eye-opening surprises. The third time she spent the night with me in Baltimore was a weekday, and I was *in furor scribendi* over some dramatic verses. At six o'clock in the morning, I sat bolt upright in our bed of love as if the fire alarm had gone off. I shook Wendy from a sound sleep and asked her as politely as I could if she would please put on her clothes and get out of my apartment for a few hours while I wrote down the lines for the poem that was seething in me. She could go to the restaurant around the corner and have a nice breakfast and coffee, and then the library would open at nine, and we could certainly meet sometime well before noon . . . .

A less confident young woman, a woman without a strong intuitive knowledge of her destined mate, might have interpreted my behavior as rejection, if not unforgivably vulgar manners toward a house guest. Perhaps Wendy had been warned about my morning compulsions, as well as my need for privacy in my work. So, being in love, she would indulge me in what seemed a fairly harmless eccentricity, as a lover might indulge his partner in a sexual whim, however kinky, taking pleasure in *their* pleasure.

But the incident must have seemed truly bizarre to her. She would tell the story again and again for many years with great humor, as a parable of my artistic obsession as well as her generosity of spirit. It probably did not make an ounce of sense to this young artist that the young poet could not scribble his verses well enough at his desk while she lay in the bed, waking or sleeping. This probably made no sense to her; yet she accepted her dismissal with a laugh, and went out for breakfast, probably amused with the premonition she would be teasing me about it for the rest of our lives.

"Our third date, and you *threw* me out of your bed at six o'clock in the morning so you could write a *poem*! Imagine! Which poem was it?"

The first year I was in college I was one of the few freshmen who had a private room in the dormitory. This was an expensive accommodation at the time. My parents did not consider it a luxury. They understood that for me, as for most Epsteins, another person's presence is a mental noise. I can think well enough when other people are around me; but I cannot study with any efficiency, and I cannot write a sentence worth reading, except in total privacy. From the day I moved in with Wendy, I have maintained a writing studio outside our home.

My wife grew up in a home that was a commune in the finest sense. She must have been astonished by my obsession for privacy, my feeling that her very presence might be an intrusion on my equilibrium. I do not think she ever understood just how much she disturbed my equilibrium, because soon after meeting her I began to act as if I could not live without her. She was getting mixed signals.

She would have to respect my privacy, honor my space, all the while we explored the joyful frontiers of intimacy. I would be happy to do the same for her. Wendy had most of the same needs, though she was more relaxed in her pursuit of them.

A few months after we met, Wendy came to live in Baltimore. Watching her set up housekeeping in an apartment and a painting studio in south Baltimore, I would marvel at her ambition, enterprise, and independence. She got herself a scholarship to the Art Institute. She began working long hours on enormous canvases of luminous abstract landscapes, paintings that reproduced in two-dimensional color the wit and passion of the woman I had first come to admire as a lover.

At last I had encountered a personality that was independently developed, different from mine in a thousand ways, that flourished in full possession of a woman equal to me as an emotional force. She did not love me any more or less than I loved her. She stood on her own two feet, glowing with health. She would love me, or some man, for a long long time, and he would thank God for it.

And although we might disagree and quarrel, Wendy Roberts would never judge me. Insofar as a judgment was ever rendered, she made it in the first hour we were together, a judgment never to be reviewed, case closed forever. I felt the same way.

There are things about me that she does not like. Chief among these is my passion for privacy, which she calls secrecy, with ill-concealed distaste.

As much as I wish to be more open and intimate with my wife than my father was with my mother, I hate to be asked where I have been or where I am going or what time I might be expected to return. I realize this may cause domestic difficulties, but I cannot help it. When the phone rings for me, I do not want to be asked afterward who called and what they had to say to me. It makes me uncomfortable to be asked what I am thinking, particularly when my mind is empty; and anyone who asks me what I am thinking when my mind is not empty, had best be prepared for the blistering truth.

When we were first married, I complained that marriage must be a prison if the inmates had constantly to be accounted for. I bridled at my wife's most innocent questions and became defensive about them, particularly during periods of erotic turmoil. I would slam out of the house, protesting that I would not be fitted with a collar and bell like a dairy cow so that my wife might more easily determine my whereabouts.

She did not like this quality in me. Such guardedness was completely unfamiliar to her and therefore unrecognizable. One of the problems in the early years of our marriage is that Wendy balked at acknowledging the distinctions between our two characters, distinctions of which I was proud. She acted as if we were identical in our needs. She would have told you, for instance, that I am no more vexed by noise than she is; the only distinction between us in this is that she is never such a crybaby about it. Likewise, she would give me no allowance for a greater innate necessity for privacy. Garbage, she would say, the man has no more need for privacy than anybody else in the family.

There may be an important sense in which she is right in these matters, but I remain loath to admit it.

Though there had been no man in her childhood home, Wendy seemed to presume that in happy families the typical husband plans his days with his wife. When he comes home from work, the good husband takes great delight in telling his wife the high and low points of his day.

I write all day, and will not tell even my wife or my best friend what I am writing until I am through with it. Often I have nothing to say about the day's work, given my self-imposed silence about my writing. Wendy could not imagine what on earth I could be doing all day that I could not tell her about it, unless it was wicked, and really she loved me too much to presume I would do anything wicked.

As for my solitary forays into the nether world of the city, from which in my restless youth I would not return until dawn, this to her seemed like insanity. I could not begin to justify it, no matter how hard I tried. After a day of solitary confinement, at age twenty-seven, I was starved for the society of a crowd—any crowd. For me the circuit of saloons and impromptu parties was a social laboratory I must explore on my own. She hated this. She swore at last that if I were not in the door by one o'clock in the morning when the bars closed, I ought not come home at all, though she knew better than to lock me out of my own house.

She hated this autonomous, private program, but she did not judge me for it. Like me, Wendy has too much appreciation for the variety of human nature to accept a putative normality and regard all exceptions as unprincipled. She loved my father while hating his manners, and would not judge him either, for she loved the good that she knew was growing in him. Wendy loved me enough to believe that my private space—which at times included the whole underworld of Baltimore City—was somehow necessary for the growth that would eventually permit the intimacy we both longed for.

We would capture it in moments, from the very first, this intimacy, this sharing. The lovemaking was a dramatic expression of it, as were the children a physical expression; but so was the sharing of dreams and anxieties, ambitions, and the pain of old wounds. When I had earned her trust, she would tell me of the difficulty of her first marriage. I would tell her how Vivian had closed the door on me forever. Wendy would unburden herself of the unending pain of losing her father, and her early memories of him; and I would tell her how my father had struck terror in my heart. Secret would lead to secret in the small, quiet hours before dawn. Intimacy would widen like a narrow path into a broad clearing, until the bright light of a new day would frighten us back into our separate forests of privacy.

This seems to be the rhythm of conjugal love as moments of intimacy lengthen into hours. After a decade of marriage, children, and shared labor, the hours of intimacy sometimes add up to an entire day of conjugal identity.

Wendy is more open than I am, though we both require

an inviolable space. I think that one of the greatest challenges of conjugal love is to inspire intimacy, but never at the expense of privacy. Conjugal love implies an invitation of one human being to another, to enter their most private emotional chambers, where they are most tender and vulnerable. But the invitation is not open-ended: you must learn when to enter and when, precisely, you must leave.

As if this were not difficult enough, you must also learn when to break into your neighbor's space when the building is on fire, or when your spouse has passed out from a leak in the gas range—all such rare occasions. In other words, you must know when silence is regenerative or therapeutic, and when it is the prelude to psychosis. You must know when to tell your wife or husband to cork the wine bottle, and when you are simply nagging.

While my wife and I are not dependent upon each other, we have, after twenty years of love, become like adjoining houses of emotion with a common parlor. Here we dance, as we did the night we met, though now sometimes we are *tout en rond* with dancing children. Here we plan the future, which for us was never a strong suit; over the years we are getting better at it. Here we celebrate, doubling our joy by toasting each other at the least opportunity, raising the crystal champagne glasses engraved with long-winged angels, the wedding gift of David Bergman. When there is no money for champagne, water will do just fine. Here we unburden ourselves of anxieties in the twilight after long days of work. For somehow there is never enough room in one house for a man or a woman's troubles, but the worries can be borne back and forth through the open doors of the two houses of conjugal love—and somehow the double space dissipates the pain. What seems to my wife an unforgettable insult or an error she may never live down, I may burst like a momentary bubble with a few words of comfort. And more than once, when I have thought my inspiration was lost forever, or that I had dishonored my name or my profession, my wife has put me back on track with her genius for humor in perspective.

My father died recently, and I thought my heart would break with the heaviness of a grief I had never experienced or imagined. I thought I would never stop falling through the darkness of my loss. More than at any other time in my life, I needed another human soul to cling to for ballast; and my wife was there for me every minute of the day and night, mourning along with me, but sane and calm in a way I could not be. I am not saying I would have fallen apart if she had not been there for me to hold. I am saying just the opposite. The point is that she held me while I grieved, permitted me to dissolve altogether in the night so I could emerge in the morning whole again. This is one of the sacred purposes of conjugal love.

Now we have been married for almost twelve years, and we have been lovers for eighteen years, most of our adult lives. The sharing is less and less voluntary, as you will see in the next chapter, because so much of our life history is the same. Though we are far too busy in the breathless tumult of the moment to marvel over the cornucopia of our memories, these overwhelm us more and more often as they increase. We give way to these memories in quiet moments when the children are asleep. I can see already that reminiscence may become a more seductive diversion as we grow older. Much that I have forgotten she recalls.

As the present relaxes its grip on us, we may find ourselves lingering at the dinner table, as the candles gutter and grow dim, remembering how the sun set in the window of that apartment in Rome, how the forsythia glowed that covered the wall on Cathedral Street, how that mockingbird sang in the sycamore, and how a particular child delighted in the sound of her own voice, singing . . .

Wendy's presence enriches my life immensely. Yet I am not dependent upon her, and I know that she would not perish without me. In twelve eventful years of marriage, we have considered divorce more than once, and once tried separation, which did not work. However difficult we found being together, we discovered that being apart was even more difficult. Now, when things are going well between us, I shudder to think what life would be like without her. I suppose she would want me to get on with it, and I would. As for me, if I should die first I hope she will find a good man to love her as she deserves to be loved, as I am just learning to love her.

If the infant tumbles into our imperfect world from a mythic paradise, it would seem to be paradise all the more because its citizens are sexually perfect, being both male and female or neither. Photographs of the human embryo reveal that the sexual organs are the last to define themselves fully in the womb.

We spend much of our energy in adulthood reconciling the male in us with the female, the female with the male, so that in the wisdom of old age we may become as integrated and sexually peaceful as an infant in the womb, or Aristophanes' man-woman in its primordial heaven.

Erotic love begins the process of integration. In the moment of possession, the ecstasy of orgasm, you are neither man nor woman; you are both as you merge with your beloved. You arise invigorated, because your partner has revived your sexual alter ego, the shadow figure of the female that inhabits every man, the shadow figure of the male that dwells within every woman. Left alone, the inner figure grows pale and lifeless; in the presence of a warm body of the opposite sex, that figure within you quickens and swells. You become whole for a time.

And the more deeply you experience this union in marriage over a period of years, the greater the impact upon your sexuality. I am fascinated by the way people who are married for decades come to resemble each other. As my grandparents got on to their fifth decade together, my grandmother became stronger in every way, taking on more of the responsibilities my grandfather had shouldered in their youth. He became more like her as she became more like him: He spent more time cooking and cleaning the house, as she spent more of her day at her job in the bank.

The wild fires of erotic love, in the controlled atmosphere of friendship, eventually transform the sexual polarity of husband and wife. After so many years of momentary physical union, and steadier and steadier spiritual union, the moments get strung together like pearls: The happy married couple at last accomplishes a complete sexual integration where the man in the woman, and the woman in the man, has triumphantly emerged. This is the purpose of conjugal love.

Conjugal love is erotic passion and pure friendship. It is erotic love with a clear vision of the future. Remember when I spoke of erotic love, I meant not only sex, because sex is only part of it. I meant a love that links the physical and the spiritual, the past and the future. In the act of making love, husband and wife are delivering each other into the future that they share.

I grew up listening to fools guffaw about the sexual boredom of marriage, and those tasteless jokes still make my blood boil. Between my own parents there was always an erotic electricity crackling, even when they quarreled: The fact is that each of them was growing and changing so rapidly one could never be boring to each other.

My parents were different every day of their lives, and noticed the changes in each other, because they were helping deliver each other into the future. Whatever their objections to marriage, boredom was not one of them.

The man or the woman you love enough to marry is not crude, supernaturally exalted, or boring, or you would not have stayed with him or her. My generation rediscovered this, and so would have little to do with an institution that smelled vaguely of the slave market, the cloister, or boiled Victorian petticoats and corsets.

Not that I have anything against the Book of Common Prayer or church weddings. I love them. I go to every wedding to which I am summoned, and I cry and laugh at the singer who sings "O Promise Me," and I toast the blessed couple in round after round of champagne, and cry some more. I got married in a church myself, or rather my wife and I did, and I still heartily recommend the setting. I like the idea of all those witnesses.

But now that I think of it, I must congratulate my parents for their courage in eloping, kicking over the table of the church wedding in the 1940s, even if what they replaced it with was a prehistoric sort of marriage.

For them at least, it was a fresh start. In their way, they were pioneers.

five

PARENTAL LOVE

Watch the little girl giving voice lessons to the parakeet, or the boy rocking the kitten and tucking it into bed; watch brothers and sisters as they comfort and advise one another—and you will notice the attitudes and tones of parental love as children reflect it.

In this they are little mirrors of their parents.

Even if a child's destiny is never to have a child of his own, he begins early to parent himself, internalizing his mother's and father's affection. I have seen my son twisting in pain from a tumble that barked his shin, talking to himself in his mother's voice: "There there, it will get better, it will be all right." And after a less painful fall, I have heard Benjamin echo his father: "Get up and shake it off, you're not hurt at all."

In the first chapter of this book, I recalled picking dandelions and violets for my mother, at age three. The scene remains vivid in my memory as the first instance of generating love on my own, demonstrating that my role in the parent-child relationship was not wholly passive.

Parental love is the ultimate human embodiment of love's

active principle. It requires a certain selflessness which appears, from the distance of childhood, unpleasant if not downright grim. But, in fact, the selflessness of parenthood proves more joyfully liberating than some parents would like you to think.

The first time my wife was pregnant, I asked my wise uncle what changes I might expect in my outlook after becoming a father.

He smiled broadly, this man who has known all the ways of love.

My uncle said, "For the first time in your life you can be sure that if you were in an open boat on rough seas, about to capsize, and there was a single life preserver—you would give the life preserver to the other human being and risk drowning yourself. There is no greater sensation of freedom."

Of course, the freedom he described is freedom from the self, and from the fear of death which haunts us from childhood when we discover death. Parenthood grants us this new freedom, as compensation for greater responsibilities for preserving life.

As we discovered in discussing erotic love, it is human nature to want good things like life and love to last forever. But, being mortal, we can go just so far in approaching the everlasting and the immortal, and then they escape us. The closest we can come to immortality is *generation,* because generation always leaves behind a new existence in place of the old one.

I always wanted children. If I had not been so busy falling in and out of love, and learning to read and write, I might have gotten a child much sooner. God knows, in the 1960s I had every opportunity. I lived through adolescence and my early twenties in the double shadow of two anxieties: that fate might deny me the sperm count I would need to increase and multiply; and that I might get some woman pregnant before we were ready to raise a child together.

I think it is common for children to fantasize about parenthood very early. I have watched the older sisters in a large young family handle their infant siblings with such ease and enthusiasm it seemed in eager anticipation of their own babies. Women have confided to me that their desire for a child preceded sexual awakening by several years—at least on a conscious level; the promptings of Eros accelerated that maternal urge to a fierce longing, usually in view of the brilliant young man who appeared to be the perfect mate.

I do not know how commonly boys fantasize in the same way about fatherhood. But I can tell you that from early adolescence until adulthood I would be swept periodically by a broad current of desire mysteriously detached from any visible object. Eventually I noticed this desire running parallel, or concurrent with, my fascination with a girl—a pretty girl with double braids in the front row of the fifth-grade class, or maybe a slender girl in a sailor blouse glimpsed in a doorway as we drove through a small town on a Sunday afternoon in the country. Fantasizing about the girl, I would desire her, surely, wanting to be alone with her in a quiet place where I could learn all about her; but there was something else I desired that was *not* the girl, that existed outside of her, around her like a mist or a rainbow. What was it? Turning the mystery over and over in my mind, I realized that the object of my perplexing desire was invisible to me because it existed only in the future, and appeared like a mist or a rainbow surrounding us because we had yet to give it a shape. The object of my desire was as yet only an idea *outside* of our bodies looking for access within us, the girl and me.

I wanted a child.

I felt the first wave of this longing when I was about nine years old, and a larger wave a year or so later. As I grew into adolescence and my midteens, this desire for a child sometimes would create in me such a high tide of longing for an hour or a day I thought my body could not contain it, that I would split into two people. Then the desire would pass. I understood vaguely what this was, and imagined having a child with Annie Berman or Cindy Myers or Rachel Honig. I talked to my mother about the emotion. I talked to Annie Berman, and she listened, fixing me with her large dark eyes, her head cocked to one side in sympathetic concentration.

Annie explained to me that all of us were feeling the same thing more or less, but we were too young to do anything about it.

This made me feel much better. And kissing helped. So we kissed.

MATING

Between the age of sixteen and my twenty-sixth year, when I finally knew conjugal love, there were three women I seriously considered marrying: Vivian Renka, Madeline Carter, and my wife, Wendy Roberts.

With each of these women I felt, simultaneous with my lust for them, the desire to father a child. The vague image of a child never disappeared from the prospect of our lovemaking; it hovered over the headboard like a symbol of our shared future.

Yet I did not have a child with anyone but Wendy. As I have told the story, our decision to have a child, our first child, looks unreflective, impetuous. I suppose it was, if you compare us with the young newlyweds who plan their children around mortgage financing of townhouses, luxury automobiles, and steeplechase thoroughbreds. But, remember, Wendy and I had known each other for five years, during the last of which we shared an apartment, meals, and chores and made love probably three thousand times before we realized that nothing could come of all this carrying on but a second generation, a baby. We possessed more love than would fit in our two bodies.

The choice of childlessness that modern birth control has offered young couples is a mixed blessing. Day to day it allows them to postpone making a choice that soon is made *for* them: Childlessness, a convenience of the moment, can become a burden over the course of a long life, if age makes childbearing impossible. There are few who do not regret it, and Wendy and I made sure not to be among them. We would plunge in feet first. Putting off the inevitable, we reasoned, would only increase our burden in the future.

On my part, there was no thought that I had found the perfect mate and mother of my children. The fact I was Jewish and she was not concerned me a little. I was punctual while she never knew the time: She was exasperatingly late, as if clocks were beneath her consideration. In fact, I was more precise and exacting about practically everything, and when I was not charmed by her easygoing ways and lightheartedness, it seemed to me like frivolity. She would lose her keys or her purse. While I am hardly the neatest person in the world, the chaos of Wendy's living quarters when I first knew her horrified me. It looked as if a tornado had passed through.

Her reservations about me must have been equally grave. I walked through doors without opening them first, and I finished other people's sentences, not always the way they had intended. Knowing what kind of man I was, headstrong, obsessive, the son of a tyrant, the gentle bride might be throwing her painting career to the wolves if she found herself suddenly with my child.

So we might not be a perfect match. But I admired Wendy's beauty, wit, and strength, and I loved being with her so much whenever she showed up that I could not imagine marrying anyone else so long as she was breathing. She must have felt the same about me. There might be another woman in five billion who could please me more, one who could tell time.

But life is short—I certainly was not going to wait around to find out.

I went to our friend David Bergman for advice on marrying Wendy Roberts. For all his admiration of Wendy, the best he could offer was the cryptic pronouncement: "Life is an adventure. Get on with it."

Insofar as I made a rational choice in selecting my children's mother, that was the deliberative process; the other part of the process, the *un*reflective part, I think I have made plain enough. I married the woman because I could not keep my hands off her. She got pregnant, by our mutual consent, and marriage seemed the only practical context in which we might raise the child.

We were poor, and neither of our careers seemed rich in material promise. So we talked about how on earth we could afford to have a family. Not much talk. There was always Mexico, and beans and rice. She would wear a peasant blouse and sandals; and I, a work shirt and bandanna. Our budget conferences fixed upon the present and the day after tomorrow. Wendy and I took all of fifteen minutes to determine that the three of us could live nearly as cheaply as two for several years, here or anywhere, and let the future take care of itself. Oh, there would be sacrifices for sure and inconvenience . . .

But who ever had a baby for the sake of convenience?

I know happily married couples, unburdened with children, who never intend to have children. I cannot pretend to understand them. I assume they enjoy the erotic bond all lovers know, and the congenial estate of pure friendship. They must experience a vital generation in nonphysical media: art, politics, spiritual growth. My dear Vivian is now a partner in such a childless marriage, and tells me she is quite happy. Maybe I will understand this kind of marriage much better when my children have grown up and left our home.

For myself I cannot imagine it. If not for parenthood Wendy and I would not have married. I have my children to thank for my marriage and the continuing adventure of conjugal love, though Wendy and I might still be lovers without a license, and true friends. We would not have married for the sake of friendship, for the two of us would have died laughing on the way to the church. Who needs to marry their friend?

We got married (and, remember, we almost did not) out of a sense of responsibility and deference to society and for the sake of our children's comfort. We thought of the little boy or girl with unwed parents, going down the school corridor on the way to class, the sidelong glances of teachers, the stupid cruelty of classmates. The child of unwed parents may still be called a bastard in 1990 as in 1890, despite our heroic campaigns upon the battlefields of manners and morals.

So we got married, the three of us, Wendy and me and the unborn baby we would call either Benjamin or Ruth, as the situation called for. The bride wore a green dress she had sewed and embroidered herself, with threads of red and gold, looking like the very spirit of fertility. I wore a white suit. We invited everyone we knew.

And they came to see us married in the little chapel of Emmanuel Episcopal Church, by a minister who agreed to conduct the ceremony the way we told him to do it, stripped of the more funereal and terrifying verses from the Book of Common Prayer. We cut out every vow that suggested we sell each other into slavery, every word that smacked of eternity, sickness, rattling chains, and death. We settled upon a few lines of romantic dialogue to the effect that we loved each other a whole lot, and would continue to love each other until we didn't any more, or couldn't.

Being Jewish, I wanted something of my tribe by which I might remember the party. So at the end of the speeches, when I had kissed my wife and hugged her and the baby within her, the minister laid an empty wine glass on the floor so I could stamp on it.

And when I had ground that crystal symbol of my past life

into the floor of the church, my new wife and I, hand in hand, ran down the aisle of shining faces, into the open weather of parenthood.

A PRIMER OF PARENTAL LOVE

For all who pay attention, pregnancy is an excellent primer of parental love.

Women must pay attention perforce: for a woman the vibration is even more commanding than erotic love, as the heartbeat of another human being comes to pound rapidly within her body. But the husband who has any power of imagination, and is as much in love with his wife as I am, begins to feel pregnant himself. Though I did not actually experience it, I have heard that some husbands are so sympathetic they suffer morning sickness in the early months of the pregnancy they have helped to bring about.

Men and women undergo dramatic changes in the nine months before the birth of a child, and the woman's bodily change is only the tip of the iceberg. The photograph of a healthy woman in her third trimester speaks volumes. But only an endocrinologist could describe the sophisticated hormonal changes underlying that magnificent sculpture, and only a psychiatrist could explain the connection between the secretion of hormones and the evolution of personality as a girl becomes a woman, or a childless woman becomes a mother. Any man in love with his wife observes this evolution during pregnancy. Under her influence he undergoes a parallel transformation of his psyche.

Before my wife knew she was pregnant, during the very first days after conception she took to her bed. She got out her knitting needles, and with hysterical concentration she began to knit some unidentifiable garment. She whistled and sang. She was not sick, she felt fine although a little warm to the touch on her forehead. But I have never seen her any busier, as if the stitches of yarn were an outer expression of the cells of the infant multiplying within her womb. She did the exact same thing when she was conceiving our second child, Benjamin.

My wife, who had always been an easygoing, accommodating individual, developed a surprising sternness of manner after learning she was pregnant. She became intractable in her diet, eating and drinking only what she wanted—green salads, chicken, and gallons of milk and mineral water, in the quantities she wanted, when she wanted. I think the legendary cravings of pregnant women are a statement of magnanimous necessity: what the woman needs now is for all of us, and we better see that she gets it—watermelon, rye bread, black-eyed peas, or caviar. My wife would not take a pill for anything, even an aspirin. Thank God, she was as healthy a pregnant lady as ever lived, for I doubt any doctor could have persuaded her to take medicine if she had been ill. She would not tolerate cigarette smoke, or the proximity of sizzling pork fat, or the fumes of any chemical or paint, because those things might harm our baby.

And if I should argue with my wife that what was O.K. for her should be O.K. for the baby, Wendy would look at me as if I did not know a baby from a cabbage. What was all right with Wendy Roberts was *not* necessarily all right for the baby. And the sooner I got that through my thick skull, the better for everyone.

I discovered changes in my own view of our needs, corresponding to my wife's outlook. We had little money, and no car insurance, or the medical benefits that come with regular employment. I earned what came from my books and lectures, which came and went with no regard for our wants and needs. I began to worry about these things in a way I never had in the days when no baby was in the offing. I bargained for a battered four-door Dodge Dart, so I would be able to drive my wife and child home from the hospital. I began to apply for teaching jobs so I would have a steady paycheck, which I never would have done before. I bought a fine cradle for the baby, though I could barely afford it—an eighteenth-century walnut cradle a friend in the antique trade found—because I believed a cradle that had been around that long would know how to take care of a baby.

Alone, I always knew I could scrape by with a little help from my friends and family. But with a baby? *We were the family.* What had been good enough for me would *not* be good enough for me and Wendy and the baby. Now I am not talking about a standard of living. The baby would eat what I ate, and live in the apartment where we had been living. I am talking about a standard of self-sufficiency. A childless man or woman might depend, openly or subliminally, upon other people for support; for an individual or a couple with a child, such dependence becomes intolerable.

We had this fierce drive for self-sufficiency in order to satisfy the protective instinct that was growing in us day by day.

This protective instinct came upon me suddenly. My wife never looked so radiantly beautiful to me as she did in pregnancy. In the first months her lips became fuller, even more voluptuous, a rich color of red she could not have achieved by painting them. Her skin shone. She looked to me like something so precious it required an elaborate and vigilant defense.

As Wendy entered her third trimester, and her center of gravity shifted upward she became charmingly clumsy. We joked about this, as she got out of a chair and listed to the right or left, like a tall ship in a high wind. Without thinking, I would take her arm as she mounted the stairs, so she and the baby would be more likely to arrive safely upon our third-floor landing. I installed a space heater in the bedroom so she might be warm enough if the steam radiators failed in the night. On city streets I was on my toes, pugnacious, alert more than ever while I walked as a shield between my pregnant wife and the busy street.

You would think no human drive could equal the drive for self-protection, until you become pregnant. Then the instinct to preserve the baby casts self-protection into the shade. Before parenthood I was my own future, and I guarded myself accordingly. Through the alchemy of parenthood, I began to see my child's future as more vivid than my own, and I began to guard it appropriately.

First, I thought, we must become self-sufficient. Then perhaps we might satisfy our growing instinct to protect the baby. Here is a corollary of the doctrine of love.

Childbirth is the dramatic climax of generation, in which we replace our old selves with the new. Sons and daughters become mothers and fathers. As the child must bring a turbulent variable into the family equation, this scene of the domestic drama demands to be acted upon a solid, elevated stage. Otherwise, there will be generational chaos.

The new baby is a wild card. Since no one on earth can be expected to love it as a mother or father will, the young parents must put themselves virtually beyond the reach of emotional, if not financial, debt. The very continuity of generations depends upon it.

MY DAUGHTER

My daughter, Johanna Ruth Epstein, was born at 10:13 on the night of November 29, 1976. She came into the world after a heroic labor of twenty hours during which my wife waved away all anesthesia. I know this because I did not leave her bedside until the baby was born. My wife thought it was important for herself and the baby to be clear-headed on this most exacting day of their lives.

The nurses stood by in awe. They had seen plenty of women since the sixties give birth without drugs, but never one who endured this much pain, particularly during the "transition period," the most demanding part of the agenda. Not to get too clinical, this is the spasmic movement wherein the cervix dilates rapidly so the baby can drop down and push its head through. This is actually a collaborative endeavor of mother *and* child. In the average birth this agony goes on for a half an hour to forty-five minutes during which many mothers committed to "natural" childbirth cave in and beg for the hypodermic needle.

I might have known that my wife, so tightly assembled and so heedless of the clock, would take two hours and forty minutes to complete the process of transition most women strive to finish in a half-hour, while the nurses perspired in sympathetic labor, and the doctors bit their nails, considering a caesarian section. The baby, for her part, would not drop, and it seemed the two of them had conspired to hold everyone up. Twelve years later, waiting endlessly in the foyer for the mother and daughter to descend the stairs dressed for an evening at the concert hall, I would remember the protracted transition of my daughter's birth. The young man who comes to court her had best bring along something to read.

Never having gone through the ordeal before, Wendy did not know how much pain she would be expected to suffer. Veterans of childbirth conveniently forget the pain as they speak of the labor, protecting their younger sisters from the terror. Maybe the veterans are afraid that if women knew how awful childbirth is, they would have no more babies and that would be the end of us. My wife had been told the business would be painful, and she will tell you she was not disappointed: the agony exceeded all her expectations. My mother, irrepressibly frank, says giving birth is like being torn apart, very slowly, by wild horses harnessed to either leg. As a clear-eyed witness of my daughter's birth, I would say this must be the worst pain any human can feel without losing consciousness. Only the joy of the creative act keeps the mother wide-eyed, alert.

My job was to rub my wife's back as she lay on her side, and feed her ice chips from a paper cup. I rubbed her back until I wore the skin away in spots, while she begged me to continue.

I remember the crown of my daughter's head as it appeared, finally, in the little opening—a dark bud. The table on which my wife lay, with her knees high and her cheeks puffed out from pushing, was wheeled from the labor room to the delivery room. I remember the corkscrew motion of my daughter's body as it slipped into the world, beet red and slick with the birth fluids. I remember the sound of her cry that brought tears to my eyes, as I bathed my daughter in a little basin of salt water the nurses had prepared. My wife passed out after her work was done.

I recount the scene in such detail in order to register, firmly, two significant perceptions. One is a sculptural image: the opening of a door. As I bathed my new daughter in the salt water of the aluminum basin, I had the powerful sensation that *I* had passed through a birth opening, through a door that connected the adjoining houses of childhood and parenthood. I had lived for twenty-six years in the house of childhood knowing the house of parenthood lay beyond the door, but not knowing its floor plan. Now I had passed through, I could see everything.

A similar birth canal on the far side of the house of parenthood would lead to the house of death. And there was no more reason to fear death than to fear parenthood.

The other significant perception I had on that celebrated morning is not so much an insight into parenthood as a physical understanding of infants, comforting to a new father, that is, the baby is strong, wonderfully strong.

I would advise any man with a serious interest in fatherhood to go with his wife to the hospital, to the labor and delivery rooms, and cover the event, watch the baby *work* with its mother in being born. The sheer tensile strength and resilience of the infant is awesome when you consider the body is being forced through an opening the size of its arm. Then you see the complicated business of breathing for the first time, and crying out to let you know it is alive, and where you can find it . . .

THE PROTECTIVE INSTINCT

Before I witnessed a birth, I thought infants were pitifully delicate, fragile little things that might wither and expire if handled with less than extravagant tenderness. Leaving the delivery room, I recognized that nature designed this creature to survive a wide range of circumstances, from extremes of temperature to hard knocks, and our instinctive affection would provide more than enough comfort for the infant's welfare, without our taking any hysterical precautions.

Not that I was prepared to see if she would bounce. As a parent, you become keenly aware of the delicacy of a child's upper spine, and the unfinished cranium like a geological fault, the soft spot at the crown of the head. Automatically your hand goes there to support the hanging head like a limp flower on its stem. You feel the brain with the child's sleeping future heavy in the palm of your hand.

I would walk up and down the nursery room in the middle of the night with my infant daughter, talking to her in a stream-of-consciousness about whatever I was thinking—philosophy, finance, the broken refrigerator—not sure that she understood exactly what I was saying, but then who did? Maybe she did not understand what I was saying, but I knew for certain that some day she would, very soon, and then I would give her more than equal time to answer—for she would be talking to me long after I could reply, when I had passed over into the house of death.

Parenthood presents a fascinating paradox of the ego. We first experience this paradox, or dissolution of the ego, through a child's eyes. But at that point we do not appreciate the weirdness of what has happened.

No one can grasp the paradox of being oneself *and* someone else until they have passed over from child to parent. The ego of an adult may be visualized as a closed curve on a plane surface, or as a sphere, a bubble in open space. One's ego may intersect with someone else's in love or friendship, but only temporarily as a rule.

Parenthood is an exception to the rule. In childbirth, the new soul conceived within you *is* you in part, another part being your mate. The unborn infant is not yet wholly itself until it comes to light and recognizes its independent existence. But at birth a remarkable thing occurs. The closed curve of the parent's ego breaks open ever so briefly, in excruciating pain, to allow passage of the new soul it has nurtured within.

And for the rest of your life as a parent, you live the paradox of seeing yourself *outside* the boundary of your ego: the daughter is you, but she is not you; the son who was so much a part of you, now walks abroad in the open air, carrying a part of you within him.

The ferocious protective instinct, probably the most distinctive quality of parental love, is a natural reaction to this paradox. You have limited control over this part of yourself which is more vulnerable than you are. This helpless creature, which has been a part of you, is now perilously exposed to the heat and cold, raw hunger and wild predators. However much energy you might invest in *self*-protection, the infant requires just so much more; its hunger seems worse than your own hunger, tears more bitter than your own tears, its pain an almost gothic magnification of your pain. It is the paradox of parenthood symbolized by the umbilical cord, the soul that is your responsibility without being under your control, that inspires the protective instinct. That, and your desire to love your child forever.

God forbid something should ever happen to your child.

And then, as if it were worrisome enough that the little girl is helpless, with her growing strength she becomes willful, perverse; she wants to eat the fringe of the carpet, the magnolias; she wants to crawl out onto the windowsill, pet the cactus, or bite the dog. No, no, no, you say, shaking your finger, hauling her out of harm's way. And no, no, no, she mimics, renewing her determination to court the disaster she has been denied.

My daughter is a great deal like me. She is probably more like me than anyone else in the world except my father. She looks similar, though more delicate, with the hands and bone structure of a true aristocrat. Her face has her mother's sensuality, but she has my family's dark Russian eyes. She is now twelve years old; at twenty she will look like a countess raised by gypsies, or the opposite, depending upon how well she does her homework.

Following in a time-honored Epstein tradition, my daughter spoke in complete sentences before her first birthday. We were living in Rome, where in the soft breeze of the twilight I would play the guitar and sing, after Ruth had been put to bed. I was working on a rendition of Gershwin's "Summertime." One evening, after I had sung through the verses twice, I heard an echo from the nursery: my infant daughter had learned the song from Wendy, and now sang it in perfect pitch and clarity, without a hint of any childish lisp or misunderstanding. The voice was small but perfect, like a young adult seen through the wrong end of a telescope.

I stopped singing "Summertime" because my daughter sang it so much better than I. When I got an urge to hear the song, I would just get Ruth to sing it.

That was in the spring. All that summer as we walked the streets and piazzas of Rome, and then the hill streets of the Isle of Elba where we vacationed across the street from Napoleon's house, my daughter Ruth would ride on my shoulders, her fingers tangling my hair, singing "Summertime, and the livin' is easy . . ." as people hung out of windows to listen to the beautiful voice pouring from the tiny body. And they would exclaim, as only Italians can, and applaud, saying this must be the holy spirit, or some sort of a magic trick. Ruth was fifteen months old and, at that age, sang "Summertime" like a miniature Bessie Smith.

If you do not believe this, you can ask my friend Robert Beaser, the composer. He made the pilgrimage to Elba to visit us, and he heard the miracle.

THE BATTLE OF WILLS

Like me, my daughter is willful in the extreme.

Just before her second birthday, Johanna Ruth began a series of tantrums rivaling my sister's of twenty years before. The tantrums became the focus of a disagreement about child raising that all but destroyed our marriage.

The disagreement was classic, and exaggerates those ancient paradigms of paternal and maternal love I described earlier.

Shortly after Ruth was born, Wendy and I had the inevitable argument over the feeding schedule. There are two schools of thought: the school of "command feeding" (where the child gives the command), and the school of the "scheduled feeding." You can guess which school I hailed from, and which was my wife's alma mater.

I declared we ought to establish a strict schedule, and stick to it, a schedule whereby Ruth would be fed at ten, two, and five, or whatever suited the mother and baby. I really did not care what the hours were as long as there was a routine the child could follow, so her hunger and our response would become more or less predictable. Generations of parents have learned that the schedule causes a week or two of infant screaming and maternal discomfort until the team gets accustomed to it.

My wife subscribed to the command school of feeding, which is timeless and has a single, subversive principle: When the baby screams, you get up and feed the baby. When the baby screams forty-five minutes later, you get up and feed the baby again. Advocates of command feeding do not let the child scream itself to sleep until the next scheduled feeding, for they consider this a barbarous contempt for the baby's personhood, hurting its pride and making a resentful baby. I could not persuade Wendy to adopt and execute a strict feeding schedule; and some nights I thought, when my daughter was about nineteen months old, I would murder the both of them in their beds if I ever got enough sleep to give me strength.

As I said, my daughter is willful, and by the age of two she had her parents on a string. I am only exaggerating a little when I tell you whatever the child commanded the parents performed, so everything went just beautifully so long as Ruth got her way.

By the time my daughter was two years old, her bedtime became an endless nightmare.

We lived in a five-room flat where the living room separated my daughter's bedroom from ours. When time came for bed, my wife would read to our daughter, rock her, sing to her, tuck her into the covers, and close the door. And Ruth would pop out again, like one of those cloth-covered spring serpents you jam into a box. Forced into the bed, she would explode into a heroic tantrum which would go on, literally for hours, so my wife finally would lie down with our daughter in her bed until the child passed out from exhaustion.

That was wrong. Alarm bells went off in my head, but my wife would not hear them over the child's cries.

We tried putting Ruth to bed an hour or two later, but it made no difference. The child's energy, her willfulness, were absolutely demonic. Whatever hour of the day or night we put our daughter to bed, she would not lie quiet unless my wife lay down by her side, in her bed or ours.

That is where I drew the line. I swore the child would go to bed, *on time,* by herself in her own bed, or I would go and live someplace else, with people who were sane. My daughter would go to bed when we told her to go to bed, if I had to tie her to the mattress or nail her down. This domestic problem became the focus of a debate that was not only practical but personal, psychosexual, and political. My wife began to regard my demands as if they were claims of an anachronistic male chauvinist determined to enslave his wife and daughter.

That is how we ended up in the office of the psychotherapist, who saved the marriage.

I had never been in the office of a psychotherapist in my twenty-nine years. I went to this doctor at my friend David Bergman's suggestion, because I truly thought I was going crazy. The doctor could clearly see that. After an hour with me, he suggested I bring in my wife. After hearing the two of us out, he quietly explained that the daughter had begun to tyrannize over the entire household, and a stop must be put to this madness immediately, before it was too late.

He asked if there were a lock on the child's door.

I began to cackle, inwardly, as my wife breathlessly explained that the nursery was a converted porch, without a solid door to speak of, only a rickety double door that opened out.

The therapist listened, impassive, stroking his beard.

And when my wife finished, he explained to us that the child must be locked into the room at whatever cost, practical or emotional. There had to be a door that closed. Our very lives depended upon it. We must establish a regular bedtime. And after reading and singing and the rest of the bedtime pleasantries, the child must be warned, once: If you get out of bed, we will shut the door for the night.

Wendy was appalled: He must not understand the child's extraordinary character. This child was not like other children. Ruth would throw herself out the window, or put her head through the door. She would scream a hole in her throat.

The doctor was unmoved. He might have been looking at a hat rack or a bare wall. He said: Put a lock on the door, and if that is the only way to keep the child in the room, do not open the door until morning.

I said that was just fine with me, paid him in cash, and walked out the door with wings on my heels. I went straightway to the hardware store and bought a hook-and-eye catch for the double doors. Checking to make sure they were strong enough to withstand the force of my daughter's rage, I installed the simple lock on the doors, whistling as I worked.

Ruth watched me, wide-eyed. "What's that, Papa?" she asked. I told her, and showed her how it worked. She was fascinated at first, then suspicious.

None of us will ever forget the night we locked Ruth in the bedroom. She screamed. She pleaded pathetically, battering the double doors with her tiny fists: "Please, please, please, Papa, open the *door*! . . ." She threw herself against it, crying, screaming as my wife lay beside me tossing and turning in sympathetic agony.

For myself, the screaming was music to my ears. I knew the door would win. As the girl collapsed, finally, into a little weary heap on the other side of the door, I knew this was the beginning of a new era in our house, the dawn of an age of tranquillity.

The strategy had an immediate and lasting effect on all of us, Ruth first and foremost. She got up the next day bright and shiny, making no mention of the night's ordeal, having already internalized a colossal resentment: Ruth probably has never forgiven us for the barbarity of the night's confinement. The next evening, upon going to bed promptly, she asked us please to leave the door open.

Wendy and I were both impressed with these quick results, and very grateful. Whenever Ruth gave us a hard time after that, we would just remind her of the lock on her door.

FATHERHOOD AND MOTHERHOOD

Neither of us is so extreme as I have portrayed us. Over the years the drama of parenthood has often caused us to cross over in our roles. I am not so strict or cruel, and Wendy was never so liberal and indulgent as she appears in that cautionary tale.

Yet there is truth in it.

You know what sort of family I come from. My father's word was law. When my father was absent, my mother's word was law. Their manners may have been worlds apart: she was kind and gentle, while he was abrupt and remote. While I knew my mother would love me no matter what I did, I suspected my father would love me only if I did what was right. But my mother and father never left any question about who was in control—the child or the parent.

My wife comes from a different sort of family, a family of women. Her father died when she was four years old. Her mother, a delightful, gentle artist, raised Wendy and her two sisters in an environment that seems, from all I have heard, to have been as peaceful and safe as any that could be imagined, once they recovered from the trauma of the man's death. While they were not wealthy, they were comfortable, settled in a large farmhouse called Sunnyside on the grounds of her rich grandparents' estate. The women were supported by an invisible income. There was more than enough time and love and money for the mother and her three daughters to develop a family society as close to a gynocratic democracy as any family could achieve, and the four remain proud of it, rightly so. Command feeding was the house rule forever, and many important decisions were made by simple will of the majority. Though they honored privacy, there were few secrets among them. I spent many an enjoyable hour in the cozy atmosphere of that home when all the women were in residence, and I cannot remember a single door in the house that closed, though surely there must have been a door to the bathroom.

Compare this with my parents' home in the wicked city, which my father regarded, philosophically, as an armed camp on the dangerous front of an interminable war. The nature of my father's business enforced a habit of secrecy upon the family members that did not stop at the front door. Half the time we did not even tell each *other* what we were up to. When I first met my wife, I was utterly charmed by the open, doorless, easygoing atmosphere of the Roberts commune, and I still have the fondest memories of it.

Little wonder, then, that my wife regarded my approach to child raising as harsh and tyrannical, if not lacking in affection. I said she was a marshmallow, and if she tried to apply the Roberts child-raising formula to a budding generation of Epsteins, she would have years to regret it. Ours is a wild gene, one step out of the jungle on the way to the statehouse or jailhouse: for three generations Epstein sons and daughters have required a firm hand on the reins in order to avoid untimely death or a criminal record. Force must be met with force. My father whipped me, because in late childhood and early adolescence I was as wild as a hyena. God only knows how I would have turned out if he had ignored me or substituted easy affection for brute resistance.

The Roberts children are born civilized.

As fate would have it, Wendy and I did not end up with Epsteins or Robertses, as I had feared. We got a delightful combination of the two. And after five years of exhausting experimentation, we arrived at a workable and humane adjustment, her mercy tempering my stern justice.

I am as curious about my children as any man, and as passionate to know them. I have always believed that the first years of parenting are the most important. Time invested "up front" has a huge emotional yield that cannot be matched by any amount of time spent with the child after adolescence. In childhood I missed by father, and I have never gotten over it—so I have tried to arrange my life to give me access to my children.

Hour for hour I probably have spent as much time with them as any father I know spends with his children, and I think I understand them rather well. Not so well as my wife, at least not the same way. I truly believe Wendy understands the children in ways I cannot, as she is closer to them than I have ever been, as hard as I try.

Although she solicits my opinion upon medical issues, my knowledge of their anatomy and pathology is no match for her intuitive knowledge of their health. More than once I have pronounced them healthy, sound as a dollar, when they were seriously ill. In infancy Ruth suffered from an infection that might have led to deafness if Wendy had not doggedly pursued it. Ruth was suffering from cranial pain a child cannot locate or describe, and I lost patience with her, grumbling we would turn her into a hypochondriac by sympathizing with her invisible ailments. I believe a doctor or two agreed with me before Wendy found one who finally got to the root of the problem, a dangerous ear infection which had to be treated repeatedly with antibiotics.

Wendy knows the children's limits of energy and patience, and their peculiar vulnerabilities, in ways I do not. I will keep them up at night, at the carnival or the fair, until they collapse in tears from fatigue, long after Wendy would have them in their beds. I feed them too much, or too little, in Wendy's absence. I forget their coats and hats. I will tease my son or daughter just beyond their limits of self-confidence, until the child reddens in embarrassment—I had not known she or he was so sensitive. I am not, mind you, *in*sensitive, but my wife is much more perfectly in tune. She dwells within the child's skin, or the child within hers, to an extent greater than I can imagine.

Wendy may understand the children better. I claim to understand the world better, and what the world will expect of our children. If there is balance in our parenting, I say it is because I represent the strangeness of the harsher world into which the children will venture, inevitably, from the warm circumference of their mother's love. I love them, surely. But they cannot expect me to think for them, anticipate their needs, or demonstrate a pleasurable affection for them if they disturb my dinner, my meditations, or my sleep.

As much as I love them, I can never love them as their mother does. To this extent they may perceive my love as conditional, though I do not feel it that way.

MY SON

I think parents get better with practice.

Wendy and I, during the first years we were "in the diaper pail," got a lot of mileage out of the joke that this is a task for professionals, and that parenthood is the only critical occupation for which there is no job training. We laughed about these things as one only laughs at jokes with an undercurrent of deadly seriousness, because over and over again we would look at each other in terror, when the baby's temperature edged toward a hundred and six, or the baby stopped its breath—wondering what in the name of God we had gotten ourselves into.

At age twenty-six when I had my first child, I had gotten into a situation so far beyond my understanding I was forced back upon my instincts to carry me through: I imitated my own parents. Having a strong father, I imitated my father particularly, though if you had interviewed me in 1978 I would have been surprised to hear it was my father I was imitating. I would have found the accusation disturbing.

You see, I was so keenly critical of my father's technique as a parent, I resolved in childhood never to be guilty of his shortcomings. I would be available, affectionate, and supportive. But this was an intellectual program I might take decades to accomplish; surely I would not manage it in the first years after Ruth was born. In the revolutionary tumult and confusion of first parenthood, a man has little leisure to think. I am pathetically sensitive to noise, and this drove me almost crazy when Ruth was a baby. I shouted *Silence!* and pounded my fist upon the table—and in the stunned silence, I realized from the terror in my wife's eyes it was not really me but my father who had barked the command.

He was peremptory and dictatorial. He breathed up all the air in a room. Yet I had grown so accustomed to the order and peace that came under his beneficent tyranny, I could not imagine my family living without it, or at least some measure of it. My wife's refusal in the first years to discipline our children, made my sternness seem all the worse. We were truly "playing off" each other in this, as the more I expected from the children at the dinner table, the more inclined she was to yawn as Ruth decorated the tablecloth with her mashed potatoes and peas or crawled with a dripping plate under her chair. Wendy seemed to think no harm could come of this, while I felt sure it was the road to sociopathology.

I am certain that a child should be told only once to do what he or she is supposed to do. Children are not entitled to elaborate explanations, arguments, or bribes. Get in the habit of giving "second chances" to the child, and the child will lose respect for your words—with good reason, for your command does not mean what it says. There are few disservices you can do a child any greater than to draw out the process of a parental command, through bargaining, apologies, or repetition—because the child internalizes the process forever, and will be decisive or vague as an adult because of it. The old adage vis-à-vis commands is that *once you begin to argue with a child, you have lost the argument.* And the child, of course, is the real loser.

Now I am not talking about dialogue between parent and child, which is equally important and has its own time and place. I strongly believe in free-form dialogue, argument, and interpretation, but *never* during the command. My wife and I fought bitterly over this issue until after the birth of our son.

Wendy was busy coping on the basis of her own instincts. She was imitating her lone parent, that lovely mother with such gentle manners and docile children she rarely required any method of control harsher than her affectionate persuasion, her musical voice.

But my dark-eyed daughter was no Roberts. When she had defied, goaded, and driven me past my limits, I would turn my five-year-old daughter over my knee and pepper her bottom. Whereupon my wife would gape at me as if I had committed an act of cannibalism, or worse: that I was perpetuating an atavistic ritual of male domination the twentieth century would tolerate no longer. I am still in a quandary about this issue, though I have yielded completely to my wife's point of view, which recently has become the conventional wisdom. I believe that children these days get their parents locked up for spanking them. I no longer paddle my children, though the thought passes through my mind from time to time, and my palms itch, with nostalgia.

My son, Benjamin Robert Epstein, was born on February 26, 1982.

The decision to have our second child was much more deliberate, indeed controversial, than the decision to have Ruth. We definitely wanted him as much; in a sense we had to want him more because now we knew the trouble of parenthood, and so we could not rush into it blind as we had five years before.

We never doubted we had enough love for more than one child. This is a principle of the doctrine of love: like a sublime vapor, parental love expands to fill the space of its container, a family of four or eleven. Couples who say they will have no more children because they do not have enough love to give them are either kidding themselves or have misunderstood this alchemy of parental love. This exists, *sui generis,* between parent and child, from the moment of birth. It owes nothing to anyone, and takes nothing away from anyone else.

There are good reasons for not having more children—ill health, poverty, other priorities—but a scarcity of parental love is not among them. Wendy and I argued about the second child because we were not sure we had enough *conjugal* love to carry us through, another five years, for the effective nurturing of a second child. As soon as we decided that we did, out went the birth control, and in a few weeks Wendy was pregnant.

For some reason, I remember being asked more often than before whether I had a preference for the child to be male or female. I replied without thinking much about it, that I loved the daughter and had begun to get used to her, so another daughter would be a welcome addition, while a son would be an exhilarating change for the whole family. That was pretty much the whole of my thinking on the subject of daughters versus sons. I have never quite understood the parents' legendary mania for having at least one of each.

So I must say I was not prepared for my response at the birth of my son. Whereas my daughter seemed to have slipped out all at once, my son appeared to be drawn out yard by yard like an extended bolt of fabric.

"What a *long* baby!" was the first review of Benjamin Robert Epstein by an attending nurse, followed by a chorus of little cries. "It's a little boy!" which soon became more than obvious as his distinguishing organ rose up and sprayed the whole audience with his first urination in the fresh air.

As I bathed my new son in the basin of saltwater the nurses provided, I felt like I was ten feet tall, with big muscles in my arms and neck. I thought of my father and my grandfather and my wise uncle: I was bathing the whole crew of them in the saltwater. I had a joyful and uncommon urge to go out and drive a car very fast, drink five or six beers, and beat the stuffing out of the first man who looked at me funny. Being too civilized for such displays of martial pride, I settled for buying a box of cigars which I handed out while winking, and laughing out loud, and ostentatiously flexing my poor arm muscle until it nearly collapsed under the strain.

Now I remember the story of my grandfather, in an age when natural childbirth was not a stylistic option but a necessity. The grateful father of two beautiful daughters, my grandfather was the sole attendant of my grandmother during her last labor, during which he surely had concerns more urgent than the sex of his third child.

But when the baby came out, a boy, and performed the miracle I have described at my son's appearance, my grandfather was so transported with joy he forgot what they were supposed to be doing. Leaving the boy sprawling between his wife's legs, my grandfather ran out into the dark, empty streets of Vienna, Maryland, crying, "It's a boy! It's a boy!" as if my baby uncle were the Messiah. The man had forgotten to cut and tie the umbilical cord; some gentle neighbor led my grandfather, blind with weeping, back to his wife's bed-side to finish the job they had begun, and not a minute too soon.

For better or worse, we cannot tell which qualities of a child's character are innate, and which are the result of paren-tal influence or expectations. I vividly remember my mother-in-law's first, long look at Benjamin as he lay in a portable crib in the afternoon light of the window in Wendy's hospital room. My mother-in-law, a celebrated artist, has keen per-ceptions and some clairvoyance. She observed, laughing, that this was a jolly baby indeed, with the gift of joy clearly written in his features. She was correct. I believe children are born with a certain capacity for joy, and my son is, in this, blessed beyond any of us.

So I do not think we can take credit for his happiness, though if he grows into a bitter, sour adult, we must assume some of the blame. He was, from the beginning, less conten-tious than my daughter, which I believe may be attributed to our improvement in parental technique; by the time the boy was old enough to try us, Wendy and I had gotten our signals straight: we were not to be played with. So he did not waste so much of his time, or ours, in a battle of wills, though his will is equal to Ruth's.

Near the heart of love dwells a fury, the primitive, blind fury at mortal separation. The wise and compassionate parent, in the fullness of love, can minimize the potential fury in an even-tempered child. But the best parent cannot wholly sup-press it. And then, excellent parents sometimes have furious children no amount of love and attention can pacify.

When my son was five years old, I found myself in the dark woods of a personal crisis. Deciding that marriage was a failed experiment, I packed my bags and moved downtown. Benjamin had already endured more separation from mother and father than had our daughter, for Wendy stayed with Ruth until the girl was ready for school, but she took a full-time job when the boy was still in diapers. An easygoing, agreeable baby, Benjamin had taken his mother's departure in stride, and entered uncomplainingly into his day-care program at age two.

But when I left home, the boy exploded. He had just been admitted to an exclusive private kindergarten on the strength of his charm and intelligence. Overnight, Benjamin seemed to change. He began acting out the most violent martial fantasies, building fortresses of blocks and desks in his class-room, threatening his classmates with makeshift weapons, and refusing categorically to follow directions or cooperate in any way with his teachers or the other children. He threw fits comparable to the legendary tantrums thrown by my daughter in the late seventies.

Benjamin's fury reminded me of my father's. My father's parents were divorced when he was a baby, and henceforth had almost nothing to do with him. The cause of my son's fury was similar to my father's, though Benjamin would sooner find relief. Benjamin was angry, first for being sepa-rated from his mother, though his natural equanimity (and his parents' affection) succeeded in quelling the anger for a time. But when I left home, the boy saw the primordial separation from his parents magnified by their separation from each other, and he reacted violently. After I came home a year later, he began to calm down, but it would take him two years to become himself again, even-tempered, wise, and sociable.

Few of us, if any, ever get over the fury entirely. I think of myself as being relatively free of anger, which is why there is so little anger in this book. Yet I remember being furious at my father's rude treatment of my mother. And I can recall more than once being put out with my mother because she did not understand my feelings as I assumed she must—I got angry at her for the unpardonable offense of not being able to read my mind.

As parents we face an impossible task: we must always remain imperfect insofar as we fail to exorcise the furies. If adults end up as angry as my father was, their anger fuels the children's. I suppose I have gotten over most of my rage at my father, along with my fear of him, now that he is in the grave. But if I have not, those emotions have no business interfering with the love I bear my son. Benjamin has his own unique personality, and he will have enough to do, I suspect, in getting along with me, without having my father mixed up in the transaction.

It is a terrible thing to disappoint a child, all the more terrible because the disappointment is inevitable. We work so hard to avoid it. With any effort at all, the loving parent at some point convinces his child of parental infallibility, which day-to-day events then conspire to disprove. I consider my wife, Wendy Roberts, to be as kind and considerate a parent as ever nursed a child, and an inspiration to me, but even she makes mistakes.

My daughter had a little doll, one of those miniature fairy queens made by Madame Alexander to look as human as possible without losing its precious idealization. She had strawberry-blond hair, blue glass eyes with long lashes, and those perfectly round cheeks and chin that only dolls can get away with, or certain girls before they become self-conscious about their beauty. The doll got handed down to our daughter from someone in Wendy's family, and Ruth named the doll Jessica.

Ruth loved Jessica so deeply and vigorously that Jessica lost an arm and a leg. This made the doll all the more adorable to the girl, as the doll's helplessness added a touch of pathos to Ruth's maternal affection. My daughter, being the least sentimental of children, avoided any excessive display of her passion for Jessica. So without careful consideration, a busy parent, charged with the task of cleaning Ruth's chaotic bedroom, might easily forget Jessica's place in Ruth's heart and mistake the doll for a discarded manikin, rubbish from some Lilliputian Saks or Bloomingdale's.

That is exactly what Wendy did. Wendy Roberts, who loves our daughter to distraction, who would not suffer "the winds of heaven to visit her face too roughly," swept Jessica out with the trash one afternoon when Ruth was away.

The awful thing about this story is that my wife *knew what she was doing:* that is, she knew and she didn't know. She knew who Jessica was, and she saw herself sweeping Jessica out with the garbage. Perhaps she was not sure exactly how much Ruth cared about the doll.

She certainly did not foresee that Ruth would fall to weeping and mourning when she discovered that Jessica had gone to the dump to be burned and buried, never to be seen again. That is what happened when Ruth came home to find Jessica missing from her place of honor on the toyshelf. "Mama, how *could* you?" Ruth cried. Wendy's immediate answer was that she had been completely absorbed in cleaning the child's room. Only when she saw Ruth's tears and heard her furious outburst over the monstrous act, did my wife recall that when *she* was Ruth's age, a tyrannical grandmother had stolen *her* doll and burned it, and Wendy might never get over the fury until it was passed on, or transmuted in her own heart to shame and remorse. Hard to say which of the two was more upset over the loss of Jessica—Ruth or Wendy. I know my wife was mortified, and only in conversation with me did she begin to see some trace of humor in the sins of the parents being visited upon the children.

I have done worse things. One night Benjamin was taking a bath, singing to himself, surrounded by rubber ducks and plastic steamships, splashing merrily while I stood at the sink and brushed my teeth. On a whim I filled a small paper cup full of cold water, turned and tossed it on the boy—purely in mindless fun, you see, the way you would tease a buddy in the college dormitory. And Benjamin burst into tears. "Why did you *do* that, Papa?" wailed the naked boy in his bath, shivering, utterly shocked by my strange cruelty. Then I could not comfort him no matter how hard I tried. I was as ashamed as I have ever been in my life, because I knew while I did not know, why I had done it. Of course, the deed was not intentionally mean. I had not been thinking, which underscores the depth of my motivation. There was nothing funny about throwing cold water on my son; it was cruelty pure and simple, anger transferred from some source so deep in me that I have all but forgotten about it.

One of the saddest things about parenting is that, no matter how hard we try, or how much we love them, one's children do not always turn out as we hope they will. All of us have stories, of the daughter from a caring family who winds up in the brothel, of the black sheep brother lost to heroin or liquor while his siblings win professional honors and raise happy families. The genetic code is no respecter of parents or their noble intentions. Sometimes the wrong child comes to the wrong parent, as was clearly the case in my father's childhood. Just as often, I believe, the parent in lamentable innocence frustrates his own intentions by passing on to his children the furies unresolved in his own childhood. As parents we are fated never to be wholly successful, which makes our efforts the more noble, the more satisfying when we succeed in any degree.

Wendy and I are most fortunate in having children we like, as well as love. Looking around us, we can easily see how this might have been otherwise. Our children like each other, and they like us, though we would love them if they did not. I could go on and on about my children, as any parent can, but this chapter is not about Benjamin and Ruth; it is about parental love.

And here I wish to describe the difference between my love for my son and my love for my daughter, if there is any contrast that arises from sexual distinctions rather than from the special characters of the two children, or from my own evolution between the ages of twenty-six when Ruth was born, and thirty-one when Benjamin came into the world.

JACKS, BUGS, AND SWORDPLAY

I wanted to be a better father than my father had been. It seemed to me this would take a great act of will, as I could not rely on my instincts to do much more than imitate my father's benevolent tyranny.

I had two guiding concepts from the very beginning. First, that every action I took as a parent would enter the children's psyche forever and become part of them. If I was cruel, there would be cruelty in them; if I lied to them, they would be liars; if I was kind, they would be kind; and if I loved them, they would love themselves and maybe other people. I have never interacted with the children without a shadow of me looking over my shoulder to judge the consequences of my behavior. When I have behaved badly with my children, I have hated myself for it. I am certain my own father was never so vigilantly reflective in his parenting.

My second thought may surprise you, because it worried me so terribly: if I had children, I would have to get down on the floor with them.

My father never got down on the floor with me, and I missed it. But now I hated the idea for myself.

I was so worried about this, when Ruth was still in the cradle, I went to my wise uncle to present my case. He puffed on his pipe thoughtfully. He had been a more studious father than my own, more careful, taking one day with another, though I would not trade my father for anybody's; but I could trust my wise uncle to give me the best advice about parental technique.

I told my wise uncle that the child would be down on the floor soon, crawling or toddling, and could not possibly come up to where I was. Where would we meet, I asked plaintively, when the child came to me with a maimed cricket, or a spinning top, or a little wagon, wanting me to join in some game or study that required lateral movement on the same plane?

How could I not appear to reject the child unless I got down on the floor? This was a physical problem with serious metaphysical implications.

The wise uncle nodded, in total understanding and grave sympathy, for he is enough like me and all of mankind to have had an identical problem. He had been an active, restless boy who grew up to be a professional baseball player. From the time he walked upright, the man never played on the floor in his life.

"I could never do it," he said sadly, no doubt recollecting his children's disappointment. "Too hard on the knees."

Wendy and I took natural childbirth classes together, in order to learn how to have our babies naturally. This was a riot, all these young and middle-aged couples in various stages of pregnancy sprawled on the floor hyperventilating, and massaging one another, and making jungle noises that dissolved in laughter. And I noticed something I remembered vaguely from circle games in our high school gym and dramatics classes. Women are comfortable on the floor. They lean on their haunches, they stretch out to rest on an extended arm and a padded hip. They can even sit right down on the soles of their feet, their legs folded under. This is amazing to me. Feet are to stand on. I have never been able to sit on my feet, and I am about as comfortable sitting on the floor as on a bed of nails. So were the rest of the men on the floor of the natural childbirth class, shifting their weight and grunting and groaning, favoring their knobby, aching knees and tender hips and raw ankles, while their wives lounged in luxurious comfort. No wonder the men couldn't wait to get out of there.

"So what do I do?" I asked my wise uncle.

"You do what you can do," he said. "If you really *cannot* get down on the floor, the child will know it, and forgive you."

This of course is equally true of being blind or deaf, color-blind or illiterate. No child ever bore a grudge or was scarred irreversibly because of something a parent could not, in the fullness of love, perform for the child.

So my wise uncle returned me to the parental responsibility of determining whether I could, or could not, get down on the floor to commune with my children. I discovered that I could, with definite limitations, and the child's appreciation made it more than worth the discomfort. It was almost as if Ruth were thinking, Gee, this must mean a lot to Papa if he's willing to *get down on the floor* and do it.

At a certain age each of the children required that I find a "sport" in which we might engage as equals. When I say they required this, what I really mean is that I saw the need for the sport in order to maintain mental hygiene. I am not a patient man. I am particularly not patient with small children. And though I am not easily bored, most children's games lose their charm for me after several minutes, after which I feel like poor Sisyphus rolling the rock up the hill, again and again and *again*—particularly little games with plastic people and animals marching *on the floor*. I never even played those games much when I was a child; I spent far more of my time in the trees.

With Ruth I realized I could not escape scot-free of the floor games if I wished to realize my goal of being a better father than my father. After a lot of guilt, and years of finding excuses as the child begged me to come down from my inaccessible height to spin the top, or push the racing car, or direct the miniature cattle ranch which I could manage only for a few minutes, I had a revelation.

Ruth was down on the floor in the hallway bouncing a ball and snatching up star-shaped bits of metal. I remembered with excitement how a girl cousin had once blackmailed me into a game of jacks, a sport that requires the eye-hand coordination of baseball, the grace of ballet, and the mental clarity and concentration of a Zen *koan*. I had quickly gotten hooked on the game, despite the fact I had to get on the floor to play it. And I spent many happy hours in intense competition over the ball and jacks.

I got down on the floor, to the musical accompaniment of the clicking and clacking of my knees and hips and ankles. I cast the jacks as my daughter looked on skeptically, and I balanced the red ball in my hand before tossing it so the ball would bounce to eye level.

Onesies . . .

My daughter was amazed at my carefulness, the intensity of my concentration, which, perhaps, she had never observed at such close quarters. I am so often clowning with the children she may have thought this was all a big joke. But as I picked up the jacks in a steadier rhythm, one by one, she could see I was deadly serious, as I am about any occupation that displays infinite possibilities for perfection. I was playing the game not for her but for myself, though it would be pointless in this case without her. As we played, I gave her no quarter, no advantage; and in response she became intensely competitive. At first skeptical of my somewhat old-fashioned technique, she began to borrow or steal the moves that served her, and our game became a battle royal of psychology, skill, and raw nerve.

Daily for two years my daughter and I played jacks. She was just a few years shy of adolescence. We got down in hallways, porches, stair landings, and hotel lobbies, wherever we could find a level surface and decent lighting. We played at any free hour of the day or night, while family, friends, or strangers stepped over and around us, muttering in amazement or admiration at the little girl and the middle-aged man laughing, and sweating, and shouting at each other, locked in desperate combat over what looks like a child's game but is most certainly a metaphor for the game of life.

My daughter is an excellent athlete, and we have come to play other games together—soccer, basketball, and tennis. But it was jacks, played on the floor, in which we got to know each other; and were it not for our exertions in that sport, it might have taken us much longer to find a ground of equality.

The summer Ruth and I discovered jacks, we were staying in an old farmhouse in the Green Mountains of Vermont. We shared the house and fields with a menagerie of bugs, spiders, and butterflies that for me had to be appreciated to be endured. I decided to become an entomologist. This seemed to me the perfect intersection of the modern, intellectual world of the laboratory, and the primitive world of the chase, a savage hunt. I would never load a rifle to hunt big game; but I could go in pursuit of the wily tiger moth, and my son could run by my side and learn his father's ways as sons have done from time immemorial.

"Look, Papa, a *bug*!" my son would shout, as if it had been a diamond on the wing or a flying camel. And off we would run after the creature, waving our butterfly nets. Up and down hills of high grass, and in and out of the forest, we would run after the bugs. We caught grasshoppers and leafhoppers and buffalo treehoppers. We caught red milkweed beetles, fire beetles, slender checkered beetles, and giant walking sticks. In the morning light we hunted butterflies as they grazed on the milkweed and meadowgrass—the skippers and swallowtails and painted ladies, the white cabbage butterfly and the yellow sulphur. By night the bugs came to us from miles around, responding to our appreciation of them, great moths beating at the windows to get at the lamplight. We would admit the most brilliant of moths for study.

So we let in the Hebrew moth with its wings of printed parchment, the white gypsy moth, and the white-lined sphinx. One night a tiger moth honored us, in all its radiant beauty, like some Renaissance angel drawn by Fra Filippo Lippi, with its tiger-striped upper wing and scarlet under wing: we were almost afraid to touch it for fear we might smudge its delicate colors. Some nights we would be visited by tussock moths so tame and affectionate they would perch on our shoulders or lips when we talked to them gently, or fly up in the air and come to our hands when we called to them.

Every bug we netted had to be named and studied. This was our rule. At the end of a hunt when we were out of breath from the chase, and panting, we would sit down on a rock or stump, haul out the bug book, and find the bug we had trapped in our portable bug house. This is a little cylinder of tin and screen where the bug is your guest until you have finished entertaining each other. Ben could not yet read but he got quick at finding the right picture of a bug in the book. I would read aloud the biography of the bug. And then we would let it go free.

So the boy and I got to know each other.

He learned that I am an energetic and fanatic hunter in pursuit of the beautiful, exotic, and elusive, and that his father is obsessive about books, the way life relates to the book and somehow always returns to it. And I learned that he is tireless, relentless even, as a hunter, omnivorously observant; perhaps most important, Benjamin has the most exquisite sympathy for the tiniest living thing. There is a famous story about Abraham Lincoln as a boy, coming upon a gang of roughnecks tormenting a box turtle; how, at some risk to his own safety, young Abe rescues the turtle from the mean boys. I can just see Benjamin Robert Epstein doing the same thing, not out of heroic sentimentality, but because it would be harmful to *all* of them for the turtle to suffer such cruelty.

Benjamin is a tall boy with an uncommonly regal bearing: people are always calling him "the prince," and I believe that from the time he first heard of kings, queens, knights, and medieval chivalry, he has somehow seen himself as a young hero in such a romance. He has dignity as well as an elfish sense of humor, a peculiar combination.

At age four he picked up a stick, lifted his free arm in formal balance against his sword arm, and boldly challenged me to a duel.

I picked up my own stick to cross swords with him, and we have been battling to the death ever since, across the living room, up and down stairs, over and under the furniture, all around the house and in and out the doorways in good weather. His mother has made us wooden weapons that outlast the store-bought plastic rapiers and sabers. But even the strongest homemade wooden swords we have reduced to splinters. Aunts and grandmothers back away in terror, begging us to lay down our swords, to beat them into plowshares, but still we fight on. The boy has excellent speed and reflexes, so I do not think I will kill him. I swing for his head, and he ducks under it. From reading encyclopedia articles about "the fence," he has learned the basic positions, defenses, thrusts, and counterthrusts. If he were as tall as I and the blades were steel, in a very few years he would kill me. But I am too clever for him. I intend to get him on a fencing team just as soon as a coach will take him on.

I prefer wrestling on the living room rug, as a much more affectionate and less dangerous form of competition.

Ritualized competition between father and son has been important in my family, particularly physical competition. My father taught me to box, and I remember those boxing lessons as the most joyful time I spent with him in my childhood, and a cornerstone of my self-confidence. I wish he would have found more time to exchange punches with me. The small boy identifies himself in terms of his father, and a good tussle in fun dramatizes the physical similarities *and* differences, so the boy can see where he is going, and the man can remember where he has been. Also, the play fighting gives the child a chance to act out his oedipal fantasy in the clear daylight: I am sure my son is more confident than I ever was—more physically confident at least—as a result of surviving hours of hand-to-hand combat with his father.

Of course, I would never suggest this program for any boy who did not insist upon it. Nor would I deny the same to a daughter who cried out for similar action. My daughter never came at me with a sword to separate me from my liver and lights—but if she had, believe me, I would have armed to defend myself.

I said I would try to describe the difference in my love for my daughter and my love for my son, and I am finding this difficult. But I know the difference has a great deal to do with identification. I identify more completely with my son, though my daughter is more like me in character. My son *is* me in miniature, so I am emotionally more vulnerable to him than to my daughter.

One of the chief components of parental love is *pathos*. This is a fine old Greek word that implies a suffering, grieving sympathy. Though there is nothing at all pathetic about either of my children, I am much more likely to feel pathos for my son in anticipating his heartaches, disappointments, and failures because they will more closely resemble my own. For the same reason I have less patience with the boy when he fails me. I cannot get enough distance, or objectivity, from him to separate his failures from mine. From my daughter there is always the natural distance provided by the gender gap.

Watching my wife and daughter quarrel, I can see the same dynamic at work. Mother is angry at daughter because Ruth has borrowed her mother's shoes and broken a heel, when Wendy had expressly forbidden the loan. The two of them become so furious I will have to intervene, and I am calm and cool because Ruth will never wear my shoes and break them.

PARENTAL LOVE AND FRIENDSHIP

I think it is extremely rare for parent and child to be true friends of the sort described in the last chapter—so rare as to be a freak of nature. The true friendship involves choice, which is out of the question in the parent-child relation. Friendship involves choice, as well as some measure of equality—also impossible between parent and child, at least in the first and last decades of the association.

Parent and child are so unequal in power, at the outset, that the child must experience the natural movement toward parity as a painful struggle. As the child's will delivers him inevitably to a condition of equality, the pain shifts from child to parent. My little boy approaches my place at the dinner table with my pipe, tobacco, matches, and ashtray arranged with ritualistic care. He offers this up to me with reverent eyes which tug at my heart. I am not all that fond of smoking. I never asked him to do this, but I cannot stop it. All I can do is try and show a sufficient gratitude as the boy struggles painfully to close the great gulf between us by any means he can find. This is an impulse similar to the inspiration of prayer.

I remember what my son is feeling because I felt the same thing for my father. The boy is feeling that same love shot through with awe verging on terror because I am so much more powerful than he is—though, unlike my own father, and unlike the awesome god of Abraham, Isaac, and Jacob, I have striven to appear harmless. I am not harmless, no matter how hard I work at it, and the child knows it.

When my son is eighteen, I am told, he will not give me the time of day. Then it will be my turn to bear the heavier burden of the separation.

Dialogue is the best hope for parent and child to bridge the gap—dialogue about anything, sports, bugs, or ethics. The conversation you begin with your son or daughter continues within them when you are apart. When my children speak I listen, and when they ask I answer them, except in situations where command must supersede the conversation.

The best parent conceives of his or her child as an equal in human value, and will strive to impart that sense of value to the child from infancy on. It takes the child twenty years to get the message, if the child is not gifted with preternatural insight. Most people do not begin to feel equal to their parents in the most important sense until they come home from college on vacation, or home from boot camp, or return home with a baby on their arm.

My mother and I are as close as any mother and son can be. We have worked together, played together, traveled, celebrated, and mourned together. I appreciate her company as much as anyone's, and if I have a free hour for lunch, phone conversation, or a hand of gin, she is at the top of my list of companions. But she is always my mother, she will be quick to remind me—a high office from which she can never resign in the name of friendship, though we are as friendly as can be. Although I cannot lie to her, there are certain things we cannot discuss, sexual things mostly. And this barrier of the unspeakable is one that ought not exist between true friends.

There is always the barrier of the unspeakable, between parent and child, and there is also the inequity of love.

Parental love is the ultimate human embodiment of love's active principle. I love my son and daughter with a tender intensity they cannot possibly equal. They should not, in the natural order of things—it is better so. My wife and I brought these children into the world as an expression of our love for each other, a creation they will never be called upon to reciprocate unless the natural world should turn itself inside out and all the clocks run backward. Survival of the species, growth itself, depends not upon filial love but parental love. Filial love is, and must be, pre-eminently reactive, or passive, in that the child becomes a medium of the parents' affection, the wood of the cello as opposed to the vibrating string. Few children love their parents as much as their parents love them, because love as a generative principle remains fixed upon the future. Children represent their parents' future; whereas parents, for all their magnitude, belong to the past.

I can never adequately thank my parents for all they have done for me, if I spend forty hours a week at it. They gave me life. How can I thank them for it? Or repay them? Only by preserving life for my own children and through them, can I begin to turn the balance of this debt.

Anyone who has children in order to be loved, flattered, thanked, or cared for has mistaken the cardinal purpose of parenthood. We have children *so we can love them*. No joy proves so great as the joy of active loving, which requires (for all of us except the saints) a physical medium. Children are the body without which love would suffocate and find no future for the lack of a sufficient medium.

Conveniently, our children are a generation or two younger than we are, so we can love them until we die, if not forever.

THE DOCTRINE OF
PARENTAL LOVE

When we were children—Paul, Harry, Leonard, and I, playing up and down the street, in and out of each other's houses slamming doors—my mother referred to the whole bunch of us collectively as "her boys."

I believe she was experiencing the common extension of parental love beyond her own offspring to the whole species.

Some parents are very possessive about their sons and daughters, and so protective of them they regard the neighbor's children with suspicion. This is more rare than my mother's feeling of maternal love for the good boys and girls of the neighborhood, a genuine altruism. This compassion is one step toward a kind of immortality and religious love I will be discussing at length in the next chapter.

Shortly after my daughter was born, I stopped attending the club prize fights at the Steelworkers' Hall. I had always loved the prize fights, and Wendy and I used to go and smoke cigars and watch the sweat and the teeth fly in the spotlit ring as the boxers rattled each other's brains with hooks and jabs and right crosses.

Suddenly I did not want to watch the fights any more. I always knew it must hurt to get belted in the head like that. But after my daughter was born, I could *feel* the impact of the boxer's fist on my cheekbone, my cut lip, or my swollen eye, in a way I never could have felt it before. And then the spectacle was not nearly as much fun. My daughter's flesh had become my flesh, and so to some extent had everybody else's, including the young boxer's, though I had never seen him before in my life and would never see him again.

After my son was born, I experienced a wholly unexpected intensification of my love for my father. Talking to other young men about this, I discovered it is an almost universal phenomenon. After your son is born, and you get used to holding and cuddling him, you begin to transfer that tenderness to your father if he is there, and the feeling is wonderfully pleasurable and liberating. I began to hug and kiss my father as I never had done before, and he was all for it. By the strange alchemy of parental love, I had found that I was becoming my father's father.

This made me feel an easier affection for all men.

Long before this Eros had taught me the tender affection for unfamiliar women. Parenthood, and its paradoxical erosion of the ego walls, permitted me to feel a greater tenderness and altruism for others regardless of their sex. This lesson of parenthood seems to be common, if not universal.

At the beginning of this book, I intimated my belief that the maturing of a society is like a child's growth into adulthood through experience and education. Love is the great educator. Understanding that a person experiences the ways of love in a fairly predictable order, we may likewise ascertain the degree of a nation's emotional development according to the dominant mode of love in any historical period.

Primitive societies exist for centuries in what is basically a filial mode, in which the entire culture is restrained, hobbled by the fear that characterizes a child's love for his or her parents, finding political expression in a totalitarian, tribal, and usually stagnant monarchy. In the time of Saint Augustine, Rome was at the beginning of a revolutionary spiritual mode. America during the Civil War found itself in the mode of sibling love, which achieves its highest expression in the drama of brothers and sisters fighting side by side while murdering their other brothers and sisters. When the dust had cleared, our nation entered an erotic mode corresponding to the Industrial Revolution. Despite the kinks and wrinkles of the Victorian age, the erotic mode continued well into the mid-twentieth century, but did not reach its apotheosis until the 1960s, when Eros shook the foundations of the traditional marriage and reawakened the petrified roots of conjugal love.

We are now entering a period of history in which parental love must be the dominant way of love.

I do not mean that everyone has to have children, or that

filial love, or erotic or spiritual love should languish. I mean that human sympathy—to the extent of pathos, ego erosion, and the protective instinct—must animate the human heart to a degree American culture has never before witnessed. Parental love, as I have defined and described it, must supersede all other ways of love, or we will suffer a worse fate than imperial Rome, which could not accomplish its transition from the erotic to the paternal mode.

If we do not change, our children will not be able to breathe the air, drink the water, or walk in the sun; if we do not change, our children will have nothing to breathe and eat but fire.

If we do not become the greatest parents in history, there will be no more children and no more love.

six

SPIRITUAL LOVE

OUR LOVE FOR GOD

This is the holiday season. The city streets bustle and hum with shoppers, who look into the store windows at possible and impossible gifts elaborately decorated with red and green ribbons and gilt wrapping and aluminum snow. There are designer scarves and neckties, and dressing gowns and silk blouses, diamond necklaces and racing bicycles, and baby dolls so real they nearly cry out for rescue.

A woman carrying a shopping bag moves from window to window lost in thought, gazing into the jewelry store's display. She steps back to regard her face reflected in the glass. The transparent image of her slender neck almost fits the real circle of the necklace she admires.

I bet I can tell you what she is thinking. She is thinking of gifts, the gift she wants most to purchase for her beloved, and the gift she dreams her beloved will wrap for her to open on Christmas morning. This lady is not uncommonly selfish or generous; she is just like you and me.

There is pathos in giving, as well as in receiving presents. For me this pathos remains inseparable from the joy of the exchange. I do not know how early in life I realized this, but I must have been on the receiving end when I first felt it.

When I was about seven years old, my best friend, Paul, and his sister and brother went away to camp for three weeks in the summer. Paul told me I had best keep an eye on his grandmother, old Mrs. Osborne, who was used to taking care of children and might fall to grieving in their absence. She was a queer little old lady with white hair like spun glass, who wore long, straitly cut cotton print dresses nearly transparent with age. She was hopelessly stuck in the nineteenth century, and the only useful thing she conveyed into her bewildering modern circumstances was her indomitable maternal instinct. I made a point of visiting Mrs. Osborne in the mornings, and spent a night or two with the old lady, sleeping in Paul's bed. When he got home, Paul was so grateful to me for my attentions to his lonely grandmother he gave me a cigarbox hastily wrapped with blue ribbon, which contained his entire fortune—thirty-seven pennies and a large ball bearing. This was not payment for services rendered; it was a gift of love.

My son, in the fullness of love of an entirely different pitch, comes to me with the most remarkable presents—old pencils, maple leaves, stones, scraps of metal or bright fabric he will wrap in construction paper or butcher paper for the sheer joy of watching me open the present, hearing me exclaim: "What a magnificent bottlecap! What a glorious pebble! How artfully packaged! How thoughtful of you, Benjamin, it was just the thing . . ." And he will run off to dig up something else for me to unwrap.

My heart goes out to the boy because no gift on earth, no diamond, silk tie, drawing, or poem would not be humbled by the magnitude of the emotion he wishes to express. A long embrace comes closest to bearing the freight of the emotion, but any parent can tell you that even the longest embrace is never quite enough.

Think of the millions of gifts that will be presented during the holiday season in joy touched with pathos, the yearning to express through material things an emotion that can find no outlet even in the most elegant, extravagant physical expressions . . .

Just as our love cannot be adequately conveyed by physical gifts, our heart's deepest instinct will never be satisfied by any earthly affection. This is human nature. You cannot love anyone quite enough, or be loved by them enough.

The desire to love and be loved is truly the deepest instinct of the human heart. Thoughtful men and women who have known love in all its human forms have concluded that this instinct, the *amoris desiderium,* cannot be satisfied with earthly affection but demands, at last, an infinite object and an infinite response. Human beings, alas, are all too finite, with their beginnings, their middles, and their endings—hence, the overwhelming necessity for a god to love and be loved by forever.

Gods of love are a relatively new development in the long history of religion. They succeeded the gods of fear.

When my daughter was eighteen months old, her religious instinct led her to worship the washing machine in our summer house in Elba. The washer was one of the front-loading kind we used to sit in front of in the sixties while high on hashish, watching the clothing go around in swirls of color and white bubbles. The washing machine made a terrible racket, clattering and tinkling, so my daughter was terrified all the while she was hypnotized by the psychedelic swirls of color. She named it Tinkerbell, bowed to the machine whenever it was running, and brought little gifts by way of sacrifice: her favorite stuffed animals, her books, and anything else she thought might keep the machine from swallowing *her* up and swirling her around for someone else's amusement.

"Thank you, Tinkerbell," she would say in awe and pious humility, "Thank you, thank you," backing gingerly away from the thundering deity.

Before Judaism, the Hellenic pantheon, and Christianity, there were many primitive religions whose emotional basis was in terror. Their harsh prayers and sacrifices aimed at appeasing or inspiring a God difficult to love because He or She expressed either no interest, or a cruel interest, in the congregation. The Jehovah of much of the Old Testament is, to some extent, a transitional deity from the age of the gods of fear to an age of the gods of love. And so we find in the Pentateuch the amusing spectacle of simple mortals like Jonah and Abraham arguing and pleading with the All-Mighty to be a little more reasonable, more loving and lovable, and not so infuriatingly remote and terrible.

In the New Testament it is Our Lord who does all the pleading, pleading with humankind on the one hand and God on the other to come to the table.

The Jesus who glides through the Gospels is about as lovable and unthreatening a God as anyone could imagine, though He does raise a ruckus one morning in the Temple, turning over the tables of the moneychangers in their high seats. We understand how He must have felt. Jesus is a far cry from the pagan gods "who kill us for their sport," or the God who burns the Cities of the Plain. It is much easier for people to love this new God of the New Testament than to love His Father. Yet the Father nonetheless still hovers ominously in the background of Christian thought, the ancient God of Abraham, Isaac, and Jacob, with His long and frightful history, a God who may have more important things than mercy on His Mind.

The fact is, love is not easy. While Jesus the Paraclete may intervene for the devoted Christians, bringing them a step closer to God, He may decide to do this by pitting them against the lions. The Christian must, ultimately, pay the check like the rest of us; he or she must deal with the whole Trinity, including the All-Powerful God whose effects are not always happy, kind, or even comprehensible—the God of Abraham, Isaac, Plato, and Charles Darwin.

I do not believe in atheism. I have hardly ever met an atheist who understood the meaning of the word: disbelief in the existence of God or any deity. When pressed for an account of themselves, the few of these rare humans I have met *always* revealed, sooner or later, that they were furious about some particular church that had narrowly defined the meaning of God. The priest had told them that Mr. God was supposed to do this or that; and then Mr. God never did what he was supposed to do. Or the rabbi had led them to believe that God was supposed to protect His Chosen People, and then God stood by silently as six million Jews met their deaths in the gas chambers.

Mr. or Mrs. God was supposed to behave this way or that way, and any fool, says the atheist, can see from looking at the world that there is no such benevolent or interested God. The priests and ministers and rabbis are simply making hay from the yearnings of their gullible congregations, when they are not busy fanning the flames of religious wars and persecutions.

As I said, the atheist, as opposed to an agnostic, is the angry victim of a narrow definition of the deity too often promoted by men of the cloth. In a way we can hardly blame our clergy. After all, it is difficult to talk about God. How does the clergyman talk about the immortal except in mortal terms? Very delicately, because the terms are extremely important. The first four commandments of the Decalogue were calculated to discourage idolatry—and anthropomorphism is a subtle and insidious form of idolatry. Exasperated by the difficulty of his task, the poor minister or rabbi talks of God as if He were like us, drawing God down to the human level.

The priest talks about His wisdom and His justice and His mercy, as if He were the kindest old gentleman with a beard you would ever want to meet, with arms you would happily die in, so you get to feeling good about praying to Him. And then the Old Gentleman goes and buries a hundred thousand innocent Armenians alive in one ten-second earthquake.

Of course, the budding atheist is disappointed, for he had thought any decent God would ban earthquakes or, at least, wave them on to less densely populated areas. The budding atheist responds with the righteous fury of the claimant in a class-action suit.

But who will hear his case?

If the atheist screams at the heavens that God is a big fraud, and the atheist won't believe in Him any more, or pray to Him, what good will that do the man? Who will answer him? Not the least of the atheist's problems is that he has no one to talk to but himself, and a few unqualified friends if he has any, about some matters of very grave importance.

Most of us do not define our God so narrowly, and the more thoughtful of us do not think of God in a human form. I just asked my twelve-year-old daughter what she thinks of when she thinks of God, and she said "seashells." I was charmed by this image because it is not in any way anthropomorphic. Hoping for a little more light, I asked her to elaborate. She made an arabesque motion with her hand. "You know, the wonderful shape of them."

I knew exactly. The curled shape of the large conch and chambered nautilus shells is a sublime image of infinity and perfect proportion, the famous Fibonacci spiral based upon the golden mean. This is the structural principle of much of nature, from the proportions of a beautiful human face to the growth pattern of trees and ferns, from the proportions of an architectural masterpiece to the harmonic mysteries of pure mathematics.

I thanked my daughter and returned to my writing desk,

where a large conch shell has kept me company for seven years. I bought this for her one year as a Christmas gift, put the shell on my desk, and could not part with it.

The religious impulse arises from a vague suspicion our common experience daily raises to the level of a conviction: just about everyone can agree that we are always in the presence of one infinite and eternal energy from which all things proceed. This is the common denominator of faith, and God is what everyone perceives as that "infinite and eternal energy." One is hard pressed to locate even an apoplectic atheist who will deny the existence of that infinite energy; and most reflective adults acknowledge they are vehicles, or conduits of it, as they go about their daily tasks of living and loving. Christians, when they speak of God in this way call it the Holy Spirit; Jews call it the Logos or the Law.

The question that must concern us sooner or later is whether that energy I have described is controlled by love or actually *is* love. Our question is whether the All-Great is the All-Loving.

My childhood was one long lesson in comparative religion.

My father came from a long line of Orthodox Jews; and though he had no formal religious training, he remained infused with the faith and basic principles of his Hebrew ancestors. So far as I know, he did only one thing in his life that ran counter to his instinctive Jewishness: he married a Christian.

My mother was raised as a low- or middle-church Episcopalian, and I do not believe she ever considered converting to Judaism. I know my father would never have pressured her to do such a thing because he truly believed her religion was none of his business. I agree with him.

The religion of his son, on the other hand, became very much my father's business. He began lobbying from the day I was born to make me a Jew.

Two weeks after I came into the world, my father surprised my mother by arriving home in the late afternoon, which he had never done before. He was at the head of a posse of gentlemen in black gabardine coats and beards and yarmulkes, uproariously jabbering in Yiddish and bearing whiskey bottles. One of the most ancient of the elders he introduced to my mother as Al Jolson's father, famous in his own right as a deft and impeccable *mohel*. They snatched me from my mother's arms and ordered her to the bedroom so they could perform the ancient rites of circumcision in male privacy. I think they had to barricade the door of the bedroom to keep my mother from spoiling the party, because she did not completely understand the procedure, and thought from her baby's screams that I had fallen into the hands of some satanic cult.

My mother would get even. A few days later she kidnapped me to the Eastern Shore, where the priest in the little Episcopal church subjected me to the gentler initiation of holy baptism.

In some families the mixed religious background might have become a field of conflict. In mine it did not. My mother came to admire the Jews. And when my father expressed such a passionate interest that I be educated into the mysteries of his more ancient religion, my mother saw no harm in it. She agreed to oversee my Jewish education, enrolling me in classes, driving me back and forth to lessons and services, and listening to me practice my *haftorah* and *maftir*.

She saw no harm in the program as long as I did it by choice, and as long as she might keep up her own religious practice. As a gesture of respectful interest, and for the sheer pleasure of her company, I would accompany my mother to church from time to time, familiarizing myself with the Christian liturgy.

I have written about this in some detail in the book *Star of Wonder*, and will not repeat myself here. By the time I was in my early teens, I knew as much about Judaism and Christianity as most of my friends knew about either religion. I understood their fundamental similarities and their different customs and manners. I sustained a critical admiration for both faiths.

But when my father asked me, at age eleven, whether I intended to be bar mitzvah, there was already little doubt in my mind. I would be a Jew.

Those of you familiar with *halakah,* the Jewish moral law, know that a child is not officially Jewish unless born of a Jewish mother—unless he undergoes a formal process of conversion. This was fine with me. My mother drove me to an ancient, crumbling building in Northeast Washington, D.C. Inside it looked like a Roman bath. The rabbis ordered me to take off all my clothes and lower myself into a white-tiled pool, where they dunked me ritually under the water three times as they chanted, to purify me in preparation for my new life as a Jew. My mother waited outside, and reassured me that I did not look much different than when I went in.

I did not believe then, and I do not believe now, that either religion is superior to the other. My decision expressed a temperamental and intellectual disposition—you are either a Jew or you are not; and my intense early exposure to the religion convinced me beyond any shadow of a doubt that I was a Jew.

So everything I have to say about our love for God, and God's love for humankind, comes from the vantage point of a Jew, albeit a Jew with some familiarity with the manners and theology of Christianity. If anything I say corresponds to the passion of another faith, I take no credit for it, for I profess no understanding of any religion other than these two, the faiths of my mother and father, Christianity and Judaism.

We love God, as I have described Him, because the heart's desire, the *amoris desiderium,* can be satisfied with nothing less. We cannot explain the love of anything apart from its object.

Because the notion of describing God is nearly absurd, we must resort to abstraction and metaphor in any discussion of loving Him. But if this is precise abstraction and resonant metaphor, then the discussion can serve us in contributing to the doctrine of love.

How do we love God? Is it like filial love, as I have described this, or the love of friend for friend? Is it like sibling love, with its bittersweetness? Surely the love of God could not be like erotic love or conjugal love—or could it? Since God is everything He has created, the answers to these questions are an astonishing string of affirmatives.

I love God like a father for He inspires in me an awe that sometimes verges upon fear, and because at times I have felt He would not love me if I did not do the right thing.

I love God like a mother for She can never wholly separate Herself from me, nor can She control or abnegate Her love for me.

I love God like a brother, with a bittersweetness which at times feels like pure hatred when I consider that His eternal energy permitted the Holocaust and the invention of the atom bomb.

I love God like a pure friend when I am at peace with myself in the forest or by the sea or in the concert hall, for then God and I are like a single great soul in two bodies, my body and the world's body.

I love God like a lover, for in the act of lovemaking, prayer, or any other creative act, His eternal energy coursing through me makes me tingle and throb like a cello string or the heart of Saint Theresa pierced by the arrow, though I am no saint. In loving God, I participate in immortality through regeneration.

I love God as a father loves his child, finally, because the part of His creation with which I live is pathetically vulnerable; and if I do not protect it as I would protect my own baby, there may be no more love in the world tomorrow.

All of these answers must be regarded as figurative, sheer meditative poetry. God—unlike father, mother, sister, or spouse—cannot truly be loved like any human, because God cannot be defined as a person can. Yet if we are to talk of religious love, we have no choice but to use human love as a figure, as you might use a pencil sketch to convey the beauty of the chambered nautilus on my desk. Among the more attractive features of religious love is that at last we discover an infinite object for our infinite emotional response; the downside is the difficulty of telling anyone else about it.

Everything in the world withers and dies, sadly: fathers, mothers, friends, spouses, even children (perish the thought). But God does not die. One of the ways of appreciating His eternal nature is through the love of generation, the history of the human family. The Jews make a great deal of this dimension of the Deity. They identify the individual's immortality with the eternal march of the family, the whole people, generation by generation down through the ages. . . . God is, among other things, the ongoing generations of humankind.

This is what I call "vertical" immortality, being part of an endless generation of human beings.

There is another kind of immortality perceived among contemporaries infused with a minimum of spiritual love or altruism, and I call it "horizontal" immortality. This is, quite simply, the intersection of ego bubbles that networks an entire generation enabling them to function as a social and legislative unit. Eros saw to it my own generation, the generation of the sixties, was beautifully fused, so we have every reason to expect great things from ourselves.

The appearance that we are separated from each other by our skin is an illusion that would be dispelled quickly if we had just a little more of God's intelligence. But we do not. He leaves scattered clues for us in the words of inspired poets like John Donne: "No man is an island, entire of itself . . .";

and sometimes He transmits unequivocal commands via the saints, such as the Golden Rule, "Do unto others as you would have them do unto you," which is the foundation of all human law. The latter command was first verbalized by Rabbi Hillel, a saint if there ever was one. For he had to endure the rebellious brilliance of his most famous pupil, Jeshua Ben Joseph of Nazareth, who would later say things like "Love thy neighbor as thyself," a curious piece of advice that in many cases would not be a good idea even if it were possible.

I have not known a saint, though I know they must exist, the way mathematicians can prove the existence of certain numbers or subatomic particles before actually running them down.

For the purposes of this chapter, I wish to describe a particular kind of saint, the solitary monk, going about his saintly business in some cell under a blackened Gothic church in downtown Baltimore. I think of this fellow from time to time because I believe my very life in part depends upon his assiduous practice of a form of love I experience only in scattered moments of illumination. The man is praying for me, and for you, and for all of us.

As he was growing up, one of a large family in a small town, he knew the love of mother, father, brothers, sisters, and friends. He was smaller than other children, but a normal boy in most other ways, if a bit more polite and studious, and a little less outgoing. He enjoyed his solitude more than most children, taking particular pleasure in solitary walks in the woods and fields where he might concentrate on the gigantic contents of an acorn or the complex industry of a honeybee in a wild rose.

When he was eleven years old, the boy stood at the edge of a cornfield among dry and broken stalks, watching the wild geese fly south in a skylong angle high over the salt marshes.

Suddenly a shotgun blast stunned the October air. He could see one of the wild geese begin a slow, tumbling descent toward the black river. On an inexplicable impulse the boy bent every shining ray of his formidable will upon dislodging the buckshot from the wounded wing and reversing for an instant the so-called inexorable movement of time. In the wink of an eye, the goose righted itself, spread its healed wing, and soared gracefully back toward the arrow formation that had held a place for him flying on its way south, as if nothing remarkable had happened.

Somewhere among the reeds and cattails on the far shore, a hunter rubbed his eyes and reloaded his gun, wondering if he had dreamed he killed a goose, unaware of the little saint's first miracle.

Three years later when he confided to his parents his desire to become a priest, they greeted the announcement with the mixture of pride and guarded enthusiasm good parents reserve for their young children's less practical ambitions. By the time he packed his bags for the seminary at age seventeen, there was no question in the minds of family, friends, or the church fathers that the boy had a true vocation. But they would have been astonished and deeply troubled had he been so indiscreet as to tell everyone the specific character of his vocation. For he had always been so kind, so sociable, such a comforting presence, they all expected he would return to them, after his education at the seminary, to be their parish priest, the spiritual leader of the flock.

But the young seminarian understood he was not the one man in ten thousand destined to be the spiritual leader of a community. His spiritual adviser took one look in the boy's eyes and knew what he had, though the old man had never seen it before, because the adviser's job was to know what to look for. This young man was the one in a hundred million destined to sustain by his exertions in prayer an entire wing of the house of life. He did not know he was a saint—the very idea would have frightened him; all God had told the boy was to enter a small room, get down on his knees, and pray.

When the time came for him to leave the seminary, the young saint entered the little chamber under the vaulted crypts of the great Gothic church in the heart of Baltimore, and began to pray in earnest.

Though I know something about what he prays for, I do not know how to begin to tell you what goes on inside him, which is about as simple as a nuclear reaction and perhaps more powerful.

We have all had some experience with prayer. Mine began with bedtime prayers, a comforting ritual my mother began with me as soon as I could talk. She began with the simple "God made the sun, God made the tree, God made the mountain and God made me," and when I was ready for it, she taught me the Lord's Prayer, "Our father, who art in Heaven . . ." The first is a Genesis in miniature, and the second is a true prayer beseeching God's mercy and affirming His eternal dominion. These prayers became so much an accompaniment to sleep that as a child I would not think of sleeping without praying first, particularly after learning the deceptively Gothic

Now I lay me down to sleep
I pray the Lord my soul to keep.
If I should die before I wake,
I pray the Lord my soul to take.

The prayers delivered me from the comfort of my mother's shining face, into the dark and uncertain adventure of the night's sleep, sweet dreams, and nightmares. So my first appreciation of prayer was as words of comfort for safe passage.

The saint is in his vaulted chamber under the stones of the Gothic church. He kneels facing a plain cross of unvarnished oak. The saint is praying, just getting started really, loosening up for the day's work.

Images flash through his mind: street corners, an old man in a ragged overcoat, an avalanche, a stack of papers blown by the wind through an open window. The saint got up before dawn; and although he cannot see the sun directly from his cell, the saint is peripherally aware of the declination of the sun on the horizon, as well as of the position of the planets and a few key stars. It is one of those things he has to know, that the sun is beginning to cast a faint red glow on the streets of the city above him.

He is on his knees praying, and a scarcely discernible vibration makes the pavement hum in the near vicinity of the church.

The saint's praying is like yours and mine, the way a match flame is like a forest fire, the way your singing voice is like Enrico Caruso's. All the nuns in all the convents in the state of Maryland praying around the clock for six months cannot generate the spiritual energy this guy throws off in an afternoon of routine labor, and I do not mean to disparage the effort of Our Ladies of the Sacred Heart. We need all the help we can get.

But the saint is something else again. The man is at the height of his powers, and has done almost nothing but cultivate this prodigious gift of prayer since he was fifteen years old. When he prays, God listens. If he wanted to, he could cause a giant oak to spring up instantly in the bare churchyard, or induce the mayor's glasses to shatter, suddenly, in the middle of a city council meeting. But of course the saint would never demean his gift by squandering it on such pranks and parlor tricks. He cannot afford to waste a minute of his precious time and energy on this earth. There is too much work to be done for so many people, so much suffering, so much danger . . .

Several minutes of each morning he devotes to highway traffic, the millions of motorists passing each other head on at sixty miles an hour and missing by just a few feet. A slight nod of a driver or dysfunction of a steering mechanism might cause one to crash into the oncoming traffic. On an average trip on a two-lane highway, you may pass several hundred cars, any one of which could kill you. You cannot conceivably visualize all of those people, even abstractly, or consider praying for them not to kill or be killed by the hundreds of drivers they pass, because you are not a saint. If you had his gift, and worked on it the way Houdini practiced magic or Mozart wrote symphonies, you might in a few minutes pray effectively for every driver on the highway in a particular time zone; though once in a while, being human, you would slip up. That is, you would neglect some poor soul whose cruel, untimely death might have been averted had you paid sufficient spiritual attention.

The saint gives a little less attention to air traffic controllers.

Then he may concern himself for several minutes with the breathing of newborn infants, who sometimes need help with this. Some die, of course, and there are different prayers for them. But first he must pray for those who will live, to breathe naturally. Images fly in and out of the saint's mind: a toddler on a window ledge—there, his mother catches him; a bullet speeds toward the heart of the clerk in a liquor store, and misses by an inch; another mother snatches a toddling girl from the jaws of a snarling Doberman.

The saint is concerned primarily with borderline cases, those critical human situations most likely to be turned around by the power of prayer, the near misses of automobiles, the capricious flight of airborne contagions (who will get the meningitis?), the resistance to mortal sin in the face of overwhelming financial profit. Occasionally he concerns himself with a bill in Congress, if a single vote can turn the day.

As the sun moves toward the zenith, the saint spends the last two hours of morning praying for the rich and powerful men and women of the world to soften their hearts a little, to love their children enough to make the world habitable for them. This seems like a little thing, but he knows that even with his formidable powers he may not be able to make the crucial difference. Today he spent one full hour of a very busy day praying for the soul of the vice president of a small paper firm that has been dumping chemical waste into a major tributary of the Chesapeake Bay. The vice president has three young children who have made him aware of the "environment." He has begun to avoid their eyes at breakfast, and drink heavily before dinner, because he has chosen the immediate security of his paycheck over the long-term health of his children and the immortal health of the rest of his descendents. He is considering quitting his job in public protest against his company's malevolent neglect, and the saint knows he may be able to push him over the edge . . .

And then after a ham and Swiss cheese sandwich and some mineral water, the saint spends the rest of the day, from noon until twilight, praying that none of the twenty thousand nuclear warheads in the world will go off. If you could overhear his prayers to this end, you might think he did not like God very much at all. You might be surprised to hear him arguing, with the polemical skill of a Clarence Darrow or an Oliver Wendell Holmes, confronting God angrily as if God were a wayward or thoughtless brother. If we arrive at nightfall safely, it might well be due in part to the saint's bittersweet love of God, which is really much like our own, only much more powerful.

If we cannot follow the saint's example in magnitude, we can certainly be inspired by his exhaustive love of God.

He is the spirit of altruism incarnate, completely connected to others in his passionate love of God. The saint is a perfect example of "horizontal immortality."

GOD'S LOVE FOR HUMANKIND

I began this discussion with a mystery. Now it seems fitting to end in mystery, drawing a full circle to find our end in our beginning.

About God's love for humankind, we know aboslutely nothing, though the topic is rich ground for speculation.

I am always amazed when I behold the library of theological tracts examining and re-examining mysteries upon which humankind must remain eternally ignorant. My wife's father was a theologian, and I have inherited his books and notes on Saint Augustine and Blaise Pascal, two fearless inquirers. I admire my father-in-law's affinity with these great theologians, their intellectual passion. But theology remains a discipline I have neither the time nor the inclination to pursue to its necessary conclusions, such as they are. God's ways are God's business, not mine.

Nevertheless, I remain curious about the question introduced earlier in this chapter, the question this book cannot avoid: Granted that we are ever in the presence of one infinite and eternal energy from which all things proceed, is this energy controlled by love, or is it love itself? Is the All-Great the All-Loving?

Without getting lost in the maze of theological apologies, the answer would seem to be a simple no. God is just too vast and complicated, and His creation is too full of impurities, agonies, and downright evil, for any clear-thinking person to believe that the All-Great is the All-Loving, without wrenching the word *love* out of its socket.

The word *loving* simply does not describe God's treatment of us in any way that makes sense most of the time. Look how we grow old and die, so many of us, in pain and misery. Then walk through the children's ward of any hospital. Two historical facts alone would suffice to destroy the giddy illusions of the religious optimist: the massacre of the Jews in Germany fifty years ago, and the infernal invention and stockpiling of all these nuclear warheads. Tell me this is man's mischief and not the All-Mighty's, and I must remind you that we are part of His creation from one minute to the next.

On the other hand, it is dangerously foolish to lay evil at God's door.

If you believe an All-Loving God has brought evil into the world as some sort of lesson for our benefit, or to test our faith, you are borrowing trouble. For it is just a short step from that belief to the destructive notion that evil, as well as deliverance from evil, is ultimately God's responsibility and not yours. God is *not* responsible. Responsibility is a finite, human concept engineered by and for humankind, and applying it to the All-mighty is idolatrous; it is literally playing with fire.

The All-Great is not the All-Loving, unless we have completely misunderstood the meaning of the word *love*.

So how, you may ask, do the vast majority of people in the Western world come to worship at the altar of a God they believe is all-loving, a God they believe, many of them, *is* love, part and parcel?

There are two reasons for this, which may bring us around again to the question of God's love for humankind—a very real thing, I believe—though I see God's love as diffracted, like light passing through a prism.

Religion, not to be confused with spirituality, has two broad practical functions. One is to comfort people in the presence of life's mysteries and misfortunes. The second function is to educate, to lead the congregation to a greater understanding of themselves and their common bond, to teach them to act more kindly toward friends and strangers.

Since love is the most comforting thing in the world, it is understandable that religions founded upon faith in an all-loving God would have a vast and nearly irresistible appeal. These religions appeal to our filial passion *to be loved,* and their most popular icons are the madonna with child and a God with arms outstretched to embrace the faithful.

And since love is the Great Educator, always inspiring, challenging, and pushing students along the path of wisdom, the All-Loving God provides an excellent role model for humankind. If the world is *not* beneficiary of the attentions of an All-Loving, ever-merciful deity, the preacher reasons, then it ought to be. Maybe if we just *believe* the All-Great is the All-Loving, and imitate the kind God we have imagined, then perhaps by our moral effort His creation will come around as we dreamed it; and we might realize the Kingdom of Heaven in hauling ourselves up by the seat of our pants from an earthly to an eternal paradise.

I think this is mostly well and good. I heartily support organized religion wherever it preaches true kindness and liberal understanding of *all* of humankind, not just those who happen to be gathered in a particular house of worship.

Nevertheless, we do have a problem. The problem arises, I fear, out of our intellectual or spiritual laziness, I am not sure which.

It is almost inconceivable to me that the man with thirty million dollars of net worth will not build a hospital, a school, or a shelter for the poor with twenty percent of that money he cannot possibly spend on himself. I am just as bewildered by the woman who gives the orders day in and day out at a factory manufacturing nuclear weapons, or a plant or mill dumping chemical waste into the air or water. These people sit next to me in the church and the temple. Smiling, they will warn me not to cast the first stone, because the nation is so thoroughly corrupt that every dollar is as tainted as every other; they will tell me if they are richer than Croesus, that it is sufficient charity if they employ people at a decent wage, or that they pay taxes, or that their twenty million dollars drawing ten percent interest in banks hurts no one—but I know better. I leave it to the saint to pray for such people, for I cannot figure out how to reach them.

I am no saint, and I cannot understand such a shortfall of altruism. I can only understand these people as victims of a spiritual misunderstanding. They must believe that the All-Mighty in His infinite mercy will protect them and their sons and daughters and grandchildren forever, no matter what they do and fail to do for the next generation. They must think of God as being just as kind and responsible as a good mother and father. These are cases of arrested development, men and women who have not graduated to the parental mode of human love. Like spoiled children, they expect God will take care of them and their loved ones unto eternity.

God will do nothing of the kind. And if we do not solve this problem in a few decades, it will be the end of us, once and for all.

The problem is that, for all the widespread faith in an all-loving God, most of us have little understanding of the true nature of God's grace. The faithful often overestimate it, wishfully thinking God must be omnipotently kind, while the unreligious ignore His grace altogether.

God's grace is an undeniable fact whether you believe the All-Mighty is the All-Loving or not; whether you are a Jew, a Christian, or a Hindu. Anyone who believes this concept originates in Christianity ought to reread the story of the Deluge, Exodus, and the whole Book of Job. Whatever you think of life, life is all we have, and life exists by God's grace. The world may be full of pain, and trials, and pestilence; but with the simplest exercise of imagination, anyone can imagine how much *worse* life might be. Dante did us the service a few centuries ago of imagining a thoroughgoing, flaming Hell. He described it in horrifying, imperishable *terza rima,* so we might always appreciate God's grace in making our world so pleasant, with decent temperature control, a visible spectrum, and sufficient food and water, even wine to enrich life, and a beautiful sunset now and then, or a poem or string quartet.

I am especially moved by two instances of God's grace, because I imagine our saint toiling away in his cell to sustain them.

Like all of the saint's favorite causes, these balance lightly upon the razor's edge. One is the physiology of pain, which scientists are only beginning to understand. I did not understand this at all until I watched my wife endure the pain of childbirth. Pain in a healthy body serves a therapeutic purpose, by directing our attention to a wound or an internal pressure so we may take the sensible course in healing ourselves. Upon deeper reflection, pain may be seen to have a further heuristic purpose: pain reminds us life is largely agreeable in the absence of pain; agreeably endurable in the presence of most pain; and only in rare and unfortunate instances is living so painful it cannot be endured. Suicide is a constant human option few people choose because only in unusual cases does the pain of life exceed life's pleasure, the glory of the sunlight. Those who think they have not enough courage to take their own lives ought to give themselves more credit for the bravery of living: it takes no more courage to end one's life when pain becomes unendurable. But it rarely does, by God's grace.

And when, in the extreme ravages of disease or mental illness, an unfortunate soul comes to inhabit a room or a suite of rooms in Hell, we see the most dramatic evidence of God's grace. Torturers are often frustrated by God's grace, which is continually removing the victim just out of their reach. Physicians have marveled for centuries over the dual graces of sleep and death, two angels of healing. At the bedside of cholera victims, burn victims, and cancer victims, the kind physician has mapped the geography of pain, sleep, delirium, and death. He has discovered that pain, unlike happiness, has firm borders. At a certain point of excruciation, the victims lose consciousness, and thus are delivered temporarily from their living Hell. And when one can no longer bear reawakening to the pain, the suffering soul is delivered mercifully into the house of death.

The second instance of God's grace that remains a wonder and constant source of joy to me, is the gift of love. The terrible certainty some people live in a nearly loveless isolation, persuades me love comes by God's grace, unlike the mortal breath, which suffuses everyone who lives. It makes me realize with sadness that the universe, and perhaps even human life in some dreadful form, might endure without the grace of human love as we have come to appreciate it.

God created love along with everything else—flowers, oceans, mosquitoes, and human ingenuity. He strummed the original chord I first perceived in my grandmother's house, though I was already familiar with the vibrations of individual strings—my father's love, my mother's love, and my love for them. And I had already intuited the potential for erotic love that would regenerate my spirit immortally in the flesh of my two children.

God created love. We have love by God's grace; and insofar as I can believe in God's love for humankind, it is in viewing this evidence of His grace.

The troubling thing for me, and for all of my family and friends, is that the All-Powerful in His infinite wisdom created an awful lot of things in addition to love that seem to have nothing to do with love as I understand it. I am not complaining, mind you. I will leave it to the saint to do the complaining. I am stating what I believe to be a fact despite my profound faith in God's love for humankind: the All-Powerful is not the All-Loving.

As children, parents, lovers, brothers, and friends who love one another, we have a certain responsibility, each to each and to the earth: we must become responsible parents to the earth. God created love. But God is not responsible. He gave us love, which only we can recognize, cultivate, protect, and expand—or we will put an end to the human experiment as surely as if we had given up the courage to live and gone and committed suicide, collectively. I do not believe God will lift a finger, if you will forgive the anthropomorphic figure of speech, when some fool in the White House or the Kremlin or the desert of Libya takes it into his loveless mind to blow the world to little bits. But I do believe that the saint, through his miraculous prayers, in concert with the Sisters of the Immaculate Heart and a street gang of loving protesters bearing placards, might jam the missile's delivery system.

God created love, but it is not God's responsibility. Love, and the very world that sustains it, have been left in human hands, to have and to hold.